TO REA

Also by Gavin Reid

Starting Out Together
To be Confirmed

TO REACH A NATION

The challenge of evangelism in a mass-media age

Gavin Reid

HODDER AND STOUGHTON
LONDON SYDNEY AUCKLAND TORONTO

British Library Cataloguing in Publication Data
Reid, Gavin
  To reach a nation : the challenge of evangelism in a mass
  media age—(Hodder Christian paperbacks).
  1. Evangelistic work—England
  I. Title
  269'.2'0942   BV3777.G7

ISBN 0 340 40745 X

Copyright © 1987 by Gavin Reid. First printed 1987. All rights reserved. No part of this publication may be reproduced or transmitted in any form or by any means, electronically or mechanically, including photocopying, recording or any information storage or retrieval system, without either the prior permission in writing from the publisher or a licence, permitting restricted copying, issued by the Copyright Licensing Agency, 7 Ridgmount Street, London WC1E 7AE. Printed in Great Britain for Hodder and Stoughton Limited, Mill Road, Dunton Green, Sevenoaks, Kent by Cox & Wyman Ltd., Reading, Berks. Typeset by Hewer Text Composition Services, Edinburgh.

Hodder and Stoughton Editorial Office: 47 Bedford Square, London WC1B 3DP.

For Tony and Prim Waite,

who have been good-news people

for me and for so many of us.

Contents

1	Shouting in a Dream	9
2	Christian, Secular or Profane?	25
3	All One Body?	35
4	Did Mission England Succeed?	53
5	Learning from Billy	66
6	Why isn't there a British Billy Graham?	81
7	Parables and Posters	91
8	Churches that Evangelise	102
9	Preaching for a Verdict	120
10	Electronic Gospel?	135
11	Words, Works and Wonders	147
12	Can we reach Whole Communities?	164
13	Who Cares?	180

1
Shouting in a Dream

It hardly happens to me now, but when I was a child it was a frequent and usually unpleasant experience.

I would be dreaming and find myself in the middle of a nasty situation. In one way or another I would be under threat. I would be in desperate need of help. I would try to shout. I was sure that my mouth was opening, but nothing was coming out. I would be bursting with effort and alarm and conscious that I needed help, but my shouts were smothered. The reality I experienced was that of agonised impotence.

As is often the case with childhood memories, especially the bad ones, they tend to surface from time to time and these impotent shoutings are something that I have never forgotten. Every now and then when I find myself in a situation of powerlessness and feel desperate, some inner retrieval system plays back the memory – and with the memory the feeling of despair.

What a strange way to begin a book about evangelism and the task of taking the Gospel of Jesus Christ to an entire nation! How can bad dreams have anything in common with good news? The answer to this question is all too clear to anyone with the heart of an evangelist. We believe we have good news – life-changing news. We have news that will bring people out of darkness into light. We open our mouths to speak. The effort and the urgency are there, but all too often one has the feeling that we are shouting in a dream.

The vast majority of people do not hear us, or if they do they do not hear us saying anything remotely like good news.

And yet in spite of all this I feel the situation is far more hopeful than it appears. It is more hopeful and at the same time it is more complex. Part of the despair that those of us who want to share the Gospel feel comes from not grasping those complexities.

In this book I want to show some of the complexities and to reveal how we wrestled with them in the Mission England project. We have just worked through the most ambitious and far-reaching evangelistic project that the United Kingdom has ever seen. We have seen the Christian Gospel addressed to one and a half million people at great public meetings and hundreds of thousands more through far less dramatic settings over the period of some three years.

I believe we have seen God's Spirit at work in quite significant ways. We have learned many important lessons for the future, but at the same time we have made as many mistakes. This book cannot be a triumphalist account and I shall not write in those terms. As I look back over all we have done the same task and the same challenge remain . . .

How does one 'reach a nation' with the Gospel?

This book will not be an official report either. I want the freedom to stand outside and judge. It will be a very personal document. I want to take the reader into my own perplexities as well as my certainties. I want to challenge accepted conclusions in some places and plead for a return to old paths now disdained in other places.

I shall probably make plenty of mistakes, but then as the saying has it: he who never makes a mistake usually never makes anything!

Because of this personal aspect I think it is best to take some space to show how I ended up being involved in the

Shouting in a Dream

Mission England project and to show how I have come to the position in which I now find myself.

My parents taught me to take God for granted in a positive and not a negative sense. They were not regular church-goers until my brother and I were at the point of leaving home. My father put me to bed each night by kneeling beside the bed while I said my prayers – and I think I always had something to pray about. I was encouraged to go to Sunday School and my growing activity in the Bible class and youth club at the local church met with nothing but strong approval. When my elder brother announced that he felt called to the ministry, my father seemed delighted and gave financial support through the training that was needed.

And yet his own attendance at worship was minimal at the time. I have never forgotten that. I am convinced that there are a great many people like my father. Gerald Priestland has spoken of the great number of those in the 'church of the unchurched' and I think he is right.

When I was 15 (and I still shudder at my precocity) I was very active in my local Anglican church and went with others of the congregation on a parish week-end to Hildenborough Hall in Kent. On the Sunday morning a party of us went down into the village to attend early morning Holy Communion. As we waited, hunched or on our knees for the service to begin, I was suddenly hit by the reality of what I was seeing.

Apart from the group of us from the house-party there were only one or two people present. It was the central service of the Christian Church where we are confronted with the awesome love of God. It was to speak vividly and involve us in acting out the drama of the Cross where Jesus died so that the sins of the world could be forgiven – and only two people in the local community thought it worth attending.

It was my first real experience of organised Christianity outside my own fairly flourishing suburban congregation.

As I knelt there I, who had slipped quietly into a positive faith in Christ as a boy with no great conversion experiences to look back on or point to, had my first tingling encounter with the God who speaks to and through men and women, I heard a voice speaking into me and within me. It was not my voice. It did not say what I particularly wanted to hear at the time. I can still remember the words: 'What are you going to do about it? I want you . . .'

I have never been able to escape from those words and I am ashamed to say that I have many times wanted to escape.

I knew God was calling me to full-time ministry just as my brother had been called. I went through a spell of wondering whether my role was to be that of a lay evangelist. To be honest I had dreams of addressing huge gatherings of people and calling them to turn to Christ. In those daydreams, of course, thousands heard the call and turned!

Wise advice and further thought led me through more normal channels and expressions of ministry. I was ordained deacon in the Church of England on June 12th, 1960, and began my ministry as a curate in East Ham in a lively church set in the midst of warm-hearted East Londoners.

We worked hard and tried hard. There was a flourishing youth-work and this was my main responsibility. We preached the Gospel as faithfully as we could. We were a loving congregation. We visited every house. We were ahead of the field in the degree of imagination that went into our services. I had as good a vicar (and friend) as was possible to find. We saw conversions and we saw the reconciling power of the Holy Spirit at work in a number of ways.

But we did not see congregational growth, and the impact of our work on the community at large was hard to see. They were great days and I do not think we failed, but as I look back that haunting memory of shouting in dreams returns.

A second curacy in Thames-side Essex followed. My wife, Mary, and I were put in charge of a recently-built daughter

Shouting in a Dream

church set in the middle of a shapeless mass of mainly new housing. We followed faithful ministers and the little group of us who worked together for the next three years saw growth in numbers and morale. Our Family Service was started at a time when morning worship could be attended by as few as half a dozen. Within a year we saw regular congregations of thirty or forty. When I moved on, very weary after only two and a half years, we could even reach sixty on a good day and, because most of us were shift-workers, that meant that a good deal more had some sort of regularity in worship.

My successor did a fine job, greatly improving the situation. It wasn't long before the Family Service attendance touched the 100 mark. Percentage church-growth increases would have looked very impressive, but the truth of the matter was that we were still shouting in our dreams. Some 10,000 people lived in the area we were trying to reach and people were dying every day without any sure knowledge of a loving God and a beckoning eternity.

My next job was in religious publishing. I had been asked to take over a small but well-founded book, booklet and filmstrip publishing operation within the Church Pastoral Aid Society (CPAS) – an organisation that I can never thank enough.

I had never intended to move from parish work – at least not as soon as I did – but the publishing post gave me, I thought, a chance to reach far more people with the Gospel. I spent five years with CPAS and another two and a half years with Lutterworth Press. I learned a great deal about book publishing and, as usually happens, a bit of printer's ink got into the blood and has been there ever since! I still maintain links with a publishing company.

However, for all the thousands of words that we circulated to thousands of readers, one depressing fact remained constant. We were still shouting in our dreams. Publishing is a business which has to target its natural markets. The natural market for Christian literature is that containing the people who already believe. Relatively little Christian literature finds its way into the secular bookshop. There exists a whole network of Christian book outlets and those who already know, go.

Those Christian bookshops are often very well run and one result of this is that secular book outlets see no reason to compete. I came to the conclusion that as a publisher I was 'selling coals to Newcastle'. The evangelist in me was thoroughly frustrated.

Of course, there are many important uses for books and magazines within the Christian community and I have no doubts that we need Christian publishers. The fact remains, however, that Christian literature plays a very small part in the task of taking the Gospel to the wider community.

It was about this time, as I was grappling with these frustrations, that I wrote my first book which dealt with the problems of communicating the Gospel in a mass-media age. I called it *The Gagging of God*. In it I tried to show that what the churches were doing by sticking to traditional ways of communication and, in particular, by still majoring on the sermon, was effectively putting a gag on a God who wanted to speak to this generation. I tried to show that Christians were essentially introverted in the way that they organised themselves, and at the same time television and the privately-owned motor-car were radically changing society and the way that people communicated with one another.

We were now dealing with non-community man, I argued, while the churches still relied on the dynamics of face-to-face community. We were now dealing with non-literary man, I argued, while the churches still communicated on the assumption that people read and reasoned in linear fashion. Television-dominated people, I suggested, were more aware of what was going on in Moscow and Washington than in another street of their own parish. All the world's a set and all the men and women merely spectators.

The book lost me some friends and branded me in the eyes of some others as someone who was 'rocking the boat'. The thing that appeared to grate with a number of my fellow evangelical Christians was that I seemed to be pulling the rug out from under the feet of those who wanted to stand up, Bible in hand, and preach authoritatively to the crowds who were still in darkness. The irony of it all, as far as I was concerned, was that then, as now, my greatest joy is to stand up in front of a crowd, Bible in hand, and try to proclaim Christ. I believe in the efficacy of the up-front evangelist. The problem is for such a person to be up in front of the right sort of people – those who are not yet Christian.

What the churches needed to do – so ran my argument – was to see the need to encourage talented young communicators to move into the media. We needed journalists, dramatists, broadcasters and people in any corner of society where things were being said to society at large. We also needed individual Christians to see their churches less as monasteries and more as mission stations. The churches had to stop tying up the time of their members and set them free to be outreachers.

I tried to practise what I was preaching. My next book after *The Gagging of God* was deliberately written as a book of social comment with a 'futurology' slant, à la the Alvin Tofflers of this world. I tried to show the relevance of the Christian analysis of man as an inherently sinful creature and as spiritually dead in the light of his failure to respond to the social, ethical and ecological challenges of the times. I called it *The Elaborate Funeral*. The book was a failure. To be frank, I don't think it was good enough in the first place, although it did get a fair review in *The Times Literary Supplement*. It was clear to me that the real problem with the book was that it fell between two markets. It was a book that was aimed at the worldly reader, but the publisher knew I was known as an author only in the Christian market.

It didn't particularly appeal to the Christian readership, who tend to be escapist in their tastes, and it was never seen in the secular bookshops. Once again I was shouting in a dream.

In 1974 I returned to the staff of the CPAS, this time to start up a department for evangelism. My task was to set up a resourcing service for parish churches that wanted help with their evangelism. I drove thousands of miles around the country visiting every sort of church imaginable from flourishing parochial empires to damp, tatty inner-city, museum-pieces that were a drain on the meagre resources of their heroic little congregations.

I set up parish missions, and I noted the lessons to be learned wherever things were right or went wrong. I tried to advise vicars and parochial church councillors on approaches to continuous local church evangelism.

It was my clear conviction that evangelism was best done either at a very small and personal level or on a very large scale. People tended to relate at those two dimensions. They related to family and neighbours (although this could not always be guaranteed). They related to those they worked beside and they related to people who took part in the same leisure pursuits. Apart from that they related, albeit in a different manner, to TV personalities and the people they read about in their newspapers or saw on their television screens.

Far too much of our set-piece envangelism took place in the no man's land in between. The united churches' mission in the local town hall usually turned out to be a rally of the keener members of the participating churches – more shouting in more dreams.

From this I could see the value of local churches naturally reaching out within their neighbourhoods and to the personal

Shouting in a Dream

friends of those who already came. A church could see itself as a 'flock' surrounded by a 'fringe'. The fringe could be analysed and broken down into two sorts. There was the institutional fringe, made up of those within the locality who had a tentative relationship with the activities of the church. There was the personal fringe, made up of those who were friends of those who came.

I concentrated my advice and my strategies on helping churches to identify those who were on their fringes and to finding ways of setting up unthreatening evangelistic encounters. I set out my ideas in another little book, entitled *Good News to Share*. In all this, however, I could see the desperate need to do something that also worked at the large nationwide end of the scale. We needed to set up something that took the Gospel into the world of the newspaper and television-news report. I felt that the churches were concentrating only on evangelism at the local level and totally forgetting that people today also live within this electronic and media 'community'. What is more to the point, many people consider a mark of reality and importance to be exposure in the media. The Gospel was getting all too little exposure at that level.

While all these thoughts were simmering in my mind I became aware of moves to invite Billy Graham, the American evangelist, back to London.

When Billy had come to London in 1954 he could not have found a more fervent supporter than I had been. I had prayed for the Greater London Crusade for nearly two years before it happened. I had talked to people on buses and over the refectory table at my London University college. I showed them pictures of Billy Graham meetings with huge crowds listening to the Gospel and I had read everything there was to read about the young American evangelist. I enrolled as a steward (my studies prevented my attending counsellor training-classes). I was in the college drama society at the time of the crusade and I had managed to get an entire bus-load of members along to one of the meetings.

I believe that those twelve weeks of exhausting activity in Harringay Arena made a lasting impact on England. When I later went to that East London parish there were several converts from Harringay in the congregation.

Billy Graham led another major London-based crusade in 1966 (followed by a further one-week project a year later in the same place – Earls Court). The crowds had been impressive on both occasions, and this time I was deeply involved as a counselling 'advisor' and behind the scenes in the designation room where we tried to place new converts who had no church links with a congregation where they would, please God, feel at home.

As with many others I had come to feel that the crusades of the 'sixties had failed to make the impact of 1954. I still admired Billy himself and believed him to be the finest and most gifted evangelist of this century. The question that was taxing many of my fellow evangelicals – the types of Christian who would most readily support Billy – was whether the large crusade had become an outdated strategy for reaching beyond the churches. Again others were arguing that the Graham team were wedded to an American cultural feel that was not appropriate for Britain in the 'seventies.

My own reactions to the prospect of another London crusade were different and more difficult to explain. I felt that the critics were wrong, although I could see some truth in the cultural objections. Where I differed from those wanting Billy back was that I felt they were thinking too small.

Another crusade in London was just that – another crusade in London. It would not be news. It would disappear without a trace in the middle of a mass community that hardly communicated within itself. The national newspapers might carry a couple of stories at the start, but that would be all.

Shouting in a Dream

At the end of December 1975 I set out my alternative agenda for Billy. Why not think less in terms of another crusade and more in terms of a Good News Year, I argued in an article published in the *Church of England Newspaper*. Instead of bringing Billy to London, why not take him to several parts of the country? And instead of limiting our thinking to the preparation for and execution of a one-shot crusade, why not harness the crusade to concentrated evangelism and training at local-church level so that the American would be evangelising alongside many others.

Without realising it, the concept of Mission England was beginning to take shape.

At the time my words fell on deaf ears. An Evangelical Alliance working party had been formed to strategise for a national mission, possibly with Billy Graham. It had the effect of destroying all the momentum of the initiative to bring him back to these shores. I was asked to be a member of this working party and it brought me alongside my old friend Eddie Gibbs plus Brian Mills and Tom Houston. All three were later to become key people in Mission England and the thinking we did together was to prove seminal.

We thought through a strategy for evangelism that saw the regions of England as the units, within which evangelism should take place. The nation could be reached only by evangelising within each regional unit. We also saw the need to bring into our evangelistic strategy the insights of the Church Growth thinkers. We saw the need to motivate evangelism from the local church outwards rather than from the big campaign backwards. We grasped the nettle that it was unrealistic to try to evangelise a region or a nation without evangelicals co-operating with Christians of other traditions.

Because of this last point the resultant report of the working party was circulated to such bodies as the Board for Mission and Unity of the Church of England, the British

Council of Churches and the Roman Catholic Church. The report was called *Let My People Grow* and it had the temerity to suggest that the churches should actually set themselves growth targets.

One thing that the report did *not* say was that Billy Graham was central to any such national project. I believed that he was.

Nobody referred to seemed to like the report. Non-evangelicals reacted to setting numerical targets and to the basic evangelical theology that inevitably pervaded all that was being proposed. Evangelicals, for their part, were deeply divided over any thought of co-operation in evangelism with those of other traditions and also had little appetite for the attempt to introduce such 'unspiritual' notions as target figures and percentages into the Lord's work!

Let My People Grow sank with little trace, but it had created a momentum for evangelism throughout all sections of the Church. It had touched a nerve. Church leaders were forced to ask: If not this way and if not the Billy Graham way, which way should we be taking?

Dr Donald Coggan, then Archbishop of Canterbury, needed little excuse to put evangelism on the agenda of the British churches, and the Evangelical Alliance report gave him the obvious opening to bring key people together. Out of the resultant discussions the Nationwide Initiative in Evangelism (NIE) was launched, and alongside others, I was asked to join the central committee.

What was soon made clear to the group of us who met under Dr Donald English's gifted leadership was that NIE had not been called into existence to organise any sort of co-ordinated campaign. The original title of 'National Initiative' was quickly changed to 'Nationwide Initiative' to make that point. The group of us on the central committee came from different denominations and reflected very different theological positions. One thing that we could never

Shouting in a Dream 21

have done was to have agreed completely as to what the Gospel was in the first place. Working together, however, did draw us into deep friendships and helped us to see that we were not always as divided as we thought.

A doughty full-time executive secretary was appointed and we set about the task of organising a nationwide church attendance census, county support groups for evangelism and a national residential conference.

It seemed to me in all this, however, that the NIE was doomed to be little more than an encourager of talking shops. Tons of reports and documents were circulated, one or two county groups made a good try at things and the conference and census were successes, but after a couple of years it was apparent that the denominational paymasters were losing interest.

While on the central committee I had several times spoken of the contribution that I believed Billy Graham could make. Through the Evangelical Alliance, and other groups, overtures were being made to him, but it was clear that he was uncertain as to how much support another crusade might have, and he was also unclear as to whether NIE might not, in the end, come up with something effective.

In the spring of 1981 I felt that I had to make a move. I knew that Eddie Gibbs and Clive Calver (the remarkable dynamic new leader of a reinvigorated British Youth for Christ) were also convinced that Billy Graham held the key to an effective national evangelistic project. I resigned from the NIE (with mixed feelings, for I was leaving friends) and the three of us, among other mainly younger evangelical leaders, pushed for a meeting with Billy Graham.

The meeting took place on July 6th, 1981, in a stuffy hotel room in Nice, near to where Dr Graham was joining friends on holiday. Eddie, Clive and I put our vision for a multi-venue evangelistic campaign to take place in three regions of England. We shared our vision for bringing the evangelist into the regions after two years of stimulating local-church evangelism with the vision of trying to spark off more evangelism after he had finished.

I shall never forget his reply. 'If you were asking me to come and do evangelism *for* you I don't think I should come; but if you are asking me to come and do evangelism *with* you that is something quite different. I'm excited . . .'

That evening the three of us flew back to England with a feeling that history was being made. We had secured Billy Graham's promise to come and work within our concept if we, for our part, could find sufficient support within three (possibly four) regions from the churches and local Christian leadership.

For my part I thought that I had done most of what I could do and that ahead of me lay some committee work and the excitement of seeing others shape up and lead the project.

I couldn't have been more wrong! The next four years were to prove the most stressful and exhausting years of my life. They were also to prove the most rewarding. Mission England was born that day in Nice, but it called for intensive nurturing and oversight.

On Saturday May 12th, 1984, on a cold, breezy but sunny day in Ashton Gate stadium, Bristol, I went up to the microphone to address the crowd of over 30,000 people present. This is what I said.

> It's an exciting sight to see so many people here today, and it's a great delight to welcome Billy Graham back to this country – where many of us feel he belongs!
>
> As you have heard, this is the first of eight meetings here in Bristol and the first of forty similar meetings around the country, taking in Sunderland, Norwich, Birmingham, Liverpool and Ipswich.
>
> In addition to these meetings, around a hundred-and-eighty other towns and villages will be receiving quick-

Shouting in a Dream

delivery video cassettes from some of the meetings and using them as the centre-piece of public gatherings.

It has taken two-and-a-half years to get to this point and a further year of activity is planned.

Around the country many thousands of Christian people are involved.

These meetings in Bristol would not have been possible without the combined efforts, prayers and gifts of thousands of people in the South-West and in South Wales – and may I particularly acknowledge the contributions and enthusiasm of those in Wales. In spite of the project being called 'Mission England', they have shown that Christians have a higher loyalty than to that of a national name. It is entirely appropriate that Mission England's honorary chairman is a great Welshman – George Thomas, Lord Tonypandy. [Sustained applause.]

So why have we all become so involved?

We have done these things because we believe that the message of new life and hope in Jesus Christ is as vital for people today as it's ever been.

And we have done these things because we care about our country.

Bristol is a historic city and history has always much to teach us. But far more important than the history we inherit is the history we create.

What hope and meaning and purpose in life are we handing on to our children and our children's children? What values are we handing on? What basis of morality and justice?

Above all – what sense of a loving Heavenly Father will our children have, and what awareness also that every man and woman will have to stand before a holy God to answer for the lives they have lived?

We cannot pass on what we have not found for ourselves

and I pray that these meetings will help many to find the reality of God in their lives.

This morning we received a simple, personal message for Billy Graham. It reads: 'My prayers are with you as you begin your mission.' It is signed: Robert Runcie, Archbishop of Canterbury. [Applause.]

That message says it all for thousands of us!

And now it is my great privilege, and the fulfilment of a personal nine-year dream to ask you to give a warm welcome to Dr Billy Graham.

As the crowds cheered and applauded I went back to my seat. It was a very different sort of seat from that pew in a virtually empty Kentish church and those unexpected words to a 15-year-old boy; but I have no doubts that the two seats were always connected in God's mind.

2
Christian, Secular or Profane?

I spend a fair amount of my time eating in motorway service stations. This is what happened one morning at breakfast time in a service-station cafeteria near Bristol.

I was finishing my own breakfast and gathering my thoughts for the day ahead, when I looked up to see a married couple and their two lively children carrying their trays over to a table near me. They sat the children down, sorted out their various plates, stacked the trays and began to eat. The children were obviously excited and perhaps not quite on their best behaviour. Suddenly the mother lost her patience.

'For God's sake stop it and sit still!' she exclaimed.

Some months later I was sitting eating an ice-cream by the side of the River Yare, near Norwich – a favourite holiday spot of mine. A small holiday cruiser was manoeuvring into a mooring-place near where I was sitting enjoying the sun. On board was the standard British family – mum, dad and two children. The decks were narrow and as the mother attempted to go ashore with the mooring-rope she lost her footing and fell between boat and bank.

I rushed to grab her and together with another man who had been standing near hauled her out of the cold waters. The children were within earshot.

'Christ!' she gasped.

The things we say in front of our children are significant. They reveal something of our values. We have a saying 'not in front of the children'. Most parents would want to protect their children from what they consider to be harmful. Children are imitators and the words they hear us use they will, in turn, repeat.

For those two mothers – and I think they typify many parents today – blasphemy is a trivial matter.

Does this casualness about blasphemy indicate that we live in an age of disbelief? Apparently not. Whenever the public opinion pollsters take to the streets or to their telephones and ask questions about belief, they usually record that some 70 per cent of those polled claim to believe in God.

During Billy Graham's 1984 meetings Gallup conducted a poll in Merseyside to discover something of the assumptions and beliefs against which the evangelist would be preaching. To my astonishment, they discovered that 64 per cent of the non-church-goers polled answered 'Yes' to their question, 'Do you believe that Jesus was the Son of God?' Asked whether they thought that Billy Graham with his well-known message about Jesus Christ and the need to 'receive' Christ and live for him, was saying anything relevant to their lives, 50 per cent again said, 'Yes'. The same response to the same question was given to the pollsters in Bristol and Sunderland.

When the first main press conference of Billy Graham's visit was over, I went up to a reporter from one of Britain's biggest-circulation Sunday papers. 'You press men are pretty cynical,' I started. 'And I can understand why. Why then did you give Billy such an easy ride today?'

He looked at me very thoughtfully before he replied. 'Maybe after all these years we're just beginning to think that he might have something,' he said.

Has Britain become secularised? This is a fairly technical

Christian, Secular or Profane? 27

question. It means, have we ceased to conduct our everyday lives with a continuous set of reminders that we are dependent on God? Have we lost any sense of what Peter Berger has called 'the Sacred Canopy' covering all that we do?

The answer here has to be, 'Yes'. As a society we function most of the time without seeing any need to refer to God. The Church of England may still be the established church of the realm, but it is seen as a rather threadbare, once cosy rug that nobody has the heart to throw out.

There is little hostility towards the Church. Britain has seen little of the anticlericalism that could be found in some other parts of Europe. British clergy are often lampooned, frequently pitied, sometimes admired and usually ignored. Most people are glad that they exist, but don't particuarly want them to call.

The same goes for church buildings – particularly those of the Church of England. People like them to be 'there' and don't like to see them being altered or adapted.

A few years ago we decided in our own church to embark on an ambitious redevelopment project. It involved adding extensions to the existing building and constructing a carpark in part of the surrounding graveyard. The congregation dug deep into its pockets in an attempt to provide the local community with a more flexible set of buildings.

Unfortunately, the local community did not appreciate what we were doing. Letters were published in the local newspapers about the vandalising of the lovely parish church. A reporter was dispatched to find out more. He wrote up his findings in such a way as to cast us all as villains wrecking something that was precious to the whole neighbourhood. None of the protestors who were interviewed ever came to the church as far as I could see.

One can react to this in two ways. It can be seen as a load of humbug or it can be seen as people somehow finding a deep and not unspiritual chord touched and hurt. I believe it was probably a bit of both, but that we would be foolish to ignore all the possible implications. Somewhere in the subconscious areas of mind and emotion I believe many people want the traditional church and the traditional clergyman to be there – even if they have no immediate intention of making use of them. The familiar shapes are a reminder that the whole Christian set of things might just, as the reporter said of Billy Graham, 'have something'.

Society may be secularised, but I don't think that men and women can yet be described as 'secular'.

How then – if there is still this residual respect for the familiar Christian things – do we account for the increasing degree of blasphemy? Until recently my wife was a schoolteacher. One thing that she could not avoid noticing was a rapid increase in bad language and blasphemy among her pupils.

And my wife was teaching 5-year-olds.

The answer is probably along these lines. For one reason or another our country has lost all sense of the *sacred*. This, I suggest not only affects how we regard God; it also affects how we regard other human beings. Privacy and sex are no longer sacred. Everyone has 'a right to know' and the peeping Tom is made respectable by means of the telephoto lens of the press cameraman.

When nothing is sacred and nothing is precious, then everything is commonplace.

Again, we are living in an age of increasing equality in society. Earlier generations were taught 'to respect their betters'. Now we would despise such a servile attitude. Respect is a sign of weakness. We are still used to other people having power over us, but in democratic societies it was our votes that put them there and it could be our votes that will put them out. In addition to this realisation, we are used to seeing our national leaders attacked by their political opponents and by the media. As a result we have lost the habits of showing and feeling respect.

There is, I suggest, a thin line between respect, reverence and the sacred and so we blaspheme without even thinking that it is a daring thing to do. There is no fear of God.

There is also very little in our society to encourage deep thought and reflection. When 'time is money' then our working lives are geared to a pace that gives little 'time to stand and stare'. When we get home at the end of a tiring day (assuming we are fortunate enough to have work) the television (supplemented by the video recorder) is the most popular form of relaxation. We are fed on a diet of movement and change. Television is all about pictures. It appeals more to the emotions than to the mind. It is a brave producer (and there are some) who tries to make programmes which encourage thought and reflection.

Again, television is a cockpit full of competition. The different channels are fighting to gain and to hold viewers. The pressure is on to find formats that touch the lowest common denominators and have the widest appeal. Another element in the mix is cost – studio chat-shows, for example, are far cheaper than outside broadcasts or documentaries.

It all adds up to a diet of situation comedies, violent crime series, pop-music shows, soap operas and shallow newscasts. It is hardly a diet to encourage the man in the street to reflect on the deeper questions of his existence. It is my experience that those in our society who are asking the most searching questions are often the adolescents and young adults. As people marry and get caught up in the rat race and the sheer battle to have things and to pay the bills – there is little time left to ask the questions. As in the case of respect and reverence one can lose the habit of searching for meaning.

Of course, in all this I am generalising. There are exceptions to every general principle, and one thing I have learnt from my constant dashing around the country because of Mission England is that characteristics vary tremendously from region to region. Even before the influx of immigrants from the new commonwealth, Britain was something of a patchwork quilt of different types of people.

I have tried to show that some of the necessary components that the preacher needs to find in people – an ability to reflect and a readiness to revere – can no longer be taken for granted. Strangely enough, hand in hand with these trends one finds an increasing fascination with the occult whether it be at the 'soft' level of horoscopes or at the 'harder' levels of spiritism and witchcraft.

In the autumn of 1985 I led a parish mission in a northern town. One evening during the mission found me leading a small meeting in the home of a young couple. The room was packed with their friends. A couple of us shared our testimony and tried to present the essence of the Gospel. There was a short time for open questions before we broke up for coffee and chatted in ones and twos.

I soon became aware that several people wanted me to answer the same question – 'What do you think of spiritualism?' As we talked further it became clear that at least half of those had played with Ouija boards or moved tumblers round tables or attended séances. And all this in a materialistic age!

It may be my imagination, but I think I have heard fewer people of late come up with talk about 'science disproving God' or the Bible, or something along those lines. I feel that there is a growing awareness that scientific materialism and a closed and fully explainable universe view does not meet the facts of life as people find them. This does not mean that they automatically view Christianity in a more favourable light. It means rather that a large number of people are open to non-materialistic explanations. There has been for some years a growing interest in other religions. What seems to appeal to many is a religious or quasi-religious way of thinking that makes no demands on morality.

Christian, Secular or Profane?

Thirty years ago the majority of people paid lip-service at least to what was acknowledged as Christian morality. Many when asked if they were Christians would automatically point to their attempts to 'do to others as they would be done by' and expect that to be a positive answer to the question. Hypocrisy may have been rife, but (and this is little realised today) hypocrisy can be a sign of a morally healthy community. While it is personally wrong to be a hypocrite, it shows that one acknowledges that certain moral views are right and that one would like to be thought of as acceding to those principles.

Today a lack of hypocrisy is viewed as the evidence of enlightenment. 'Yes,' one says, 'I am sleeping around with several people, but I make no attempt to hide the fact!' The logic here is that the superior morality of openness makes up for any misdemeanour in adultery or fornication.

Christian morality is challenged not only by individuals on a widespread scale but also in the manner that some laws and government regulations now apply. The thing to be clear about is this. Few people are wanting to challenge the right of Christians to live as they wish to. What is challenged is the right of Christians to suggest that their view of morality is inherently right. In the moral field as in the religious field there is a great deal of tolerance but *the cardinal sin is for anyone to claim certainty*.

The offence of Christianity is its certainty. If we were willing simply to settle for being an inward-looking group who held things dear among ourselves but let the rest of the world go about its business in its own set of ways, then we should not only be tolerated, we should probably be admired.

In this atmosphere of live and let live there is a growing tolerance of those who are fascinated by evil. We live in the age of the 'video nasty'. It is relatively easy to obtain video cassettes which portray satanism, ritual murder, bestiality, violent sequences of people being eaten alive, burned alive, hacked apart by chainsaws and the like. Films in the commercial cinema often sail as close to the same winds as they dare. *Indiana Jones and the Temple of Doom*, a brilliantly-made adventure romp which claimed that it had brought back the hero to movies after years of cynicism and the anti-hero, nevertheless contained horrific scenes of ritual murder, with people having their hearts plucked out and being burned alive.

This growing fascination with evil is also found in books, including those aimed at the children's market. The whole 'dungeons and dragons' genre has given us books full of illustrations of skeletons chained to dungeon walls, blood-covered daggers, hands with horrific talons at the fingertips, witches casting evil spells and so one could go on.

I am convinced that what we are seeing is the product of the generations that have been born and grown to adulthood since the mid-1950s. Eddie Gibbs once described the present generation of parents as the first non-Sunday-School generation of adults. I detect growing anxiety at these developments from older generations who, while not overtly Christian, were raised with certain neo-Christian assumptions and have always found these to be comfortable. The problem they have in combating these developments is that they have no philosophical or ideological base to draw on. They can easily be made to appear people of prejudice rather than people of principle. They are left with a sense of perplexity and the cliché-riddled position of shaking one's head and muttering, 'I don't know what things are coming to!'

I shall discuss the state of the churches in a later chapter, but an observation needs to be made at this stage. It is impossible to view the present religious and moral confusion and to compare it with the influence of the churches in the not-too-distant past and not to conclude that somehow we Christians have 'blown it'. The 1851 census revealed that 7.3

Christian, Secular or Profane? 33

million adults out of a possible 13.5 million English adults were in church on a given Sunday. One can only ask what was being said in those churches, what was being heard and what was being lived-out before the rest of society? Even today the combined membership of the churches far exceeds the combined membership of the political parties who control the life of the nation.[1]

One thing is clear to me from my own attempts to preach and argue the Christian case over recent years. What has been 'heard' is that religion 'is a private matter'. It has never been considered respectable to try to urge one's views on others. The basic rule of every officers' mess in the armed services is that one never talks about religion or politics.

Once people accept that Christianity is a private and personal matter then it becomes a private pilgrimage. That probably described my father's position. He assented to the orthodox Christian beliefs as far as I could see and thought that they were very important. He wanted his children to share these views (as did my mother). At all times, however, the corporate aspect – *belonging* to a church as opposed to the odd, sincerely motivated attendance – was either irrelevant or unappealing.

When the challenges of secularisation came seeping and creeping through Britain, the vast majority of men and women with Christian leanings were totally uncoordinated, theologically illiterate and so diverted into materialism and hedonism that there was no stuffing for a fight and no ability to identify any enemy.

Organised Christianity must, at least, share the blame for this.

---

[1] The 1983 *Attitudes to Bible, God and Church* survey revealed that 22 per cent of the adult population of the UK claimed to attend church once a month, with 40 per cent claiming to attend at Christmas. Of British adults, 81 per cent are in touch with the churches for 'rites of passage' – religious ceremonies relating to birth, puberty, marriage and death.

This then is the situation which the evangelist now faces. Children are being born into a society where there is a fading memory of Christianity, a present greyness of uncertainty and a growing openness to rank evil. At the same time every one of those children is a developing human being made in the image of God and with whatever it is that we call a 'soul'. We all have the spiritual equipment born into us to become a child of God. We can all be reached by the Holy Spirit. This tolerance of everything except certainty which we find today is not unlike the intellectual climate of the communities where St Paul took the Gospel. If people could be converted to Christ then, they can now.

When we went into the Mission England project in 1981 I don't think that any of us thought that we should sweep the field. Until God himself rings down the curtain on human history we shall always struggle against pervasive powers of evil. What we did feel, however, was that there was everything to gain from attempting to unite as many churches and as many Christians as possible behind a project that was based on prayer and went on to encourage the sharing of the Gospel at every level.

The general public only saw the great stadium meetings and only talked about Billy Graham. The truth was that those huge gatherings were only the tip of an iceberg of endeavour. Because of that, those meetings were evidence of the power that exists *all the time* if only Christians work together and make evangelism their top priority.

3
All One Body?

As an evangelical Christian living in England one of the biggest facts of life that I have to face is that I belong to a minority group within a minority group!

Organised Christianity is a minority interest in England and the rest of the United Kingdom. However, such an undoubtedly correct statement needs to be balanced with the reminder that we live in a country made up of minority groups. If, as the NIE survey suggested, the average Sunday church attendance is in the region of 10 per cent overall, then we are talking about a very large minority indeed. On top of that figure is another 10 and perhaps even 20 per cent of the population who would claim to attend church occasionally.

To return to our rough figure of 10 per cent, another factor needs to be added. Those in that 10 per cent minority do not agree with each other! This is where, as I said, I belong to a minority within the minority. As an evangelical and someone who wants to commend Christianity to others, I have to cope with the fact that the image of Christianity that most people have is not one that reflects my position.

Evangelism is the word used to describe the activity of preaching, explaining and urging people to do something about Jesus Christ. *Evangelical* is the term used to describe a tradition within Christianity which has two main trademarks. The first is the conviction that, after the worship of

God, the first priority of Christians is to share the Gospel and to reach out to those who would not pretend to believe. The second trademark is a conviction that the Bible is, to quote the Book of Common Prayer, 'God's word written' and as such is the final authority in all matters of faith and doctrine.

Although the two words are similar and frequently confused (especially in the popular press) it does not follow that the only Christians interested in evangelism are of the evangelical tradition. Within Anglicanism there have been some outstanding evangelists, in, for example, the Franciscan order, most members of which would be described as Anglo-Catholic (High Church).

As was evidenced in the creation of the NIE, and has been seen also in some of the support for Mission England, evangelism has become a more respectable concern within the wider Church. The remarkable 1945 report, *Towards the Conversion of England*, was the product of Anglicans of various complexions. That the report, in spite of remarkable initial interest, was pigeon-holed and forgotten within a few years is probably an indication of a fact that has inhibited effective united evangelism for years.

Although most traditions within Christianity would agree that evangelism should be a continual part of the Church's life, the differences between the traditions nearly all touch on the nature of the Gospel itself. If we are disagreed as to what it is that we wish to urge on others, then we can hardly be expected to work together. More than that: if we are indeed in disagreement about the nature of the Gospel, then the evangelism of one tradition can be a disagreeable activity to Christians of another.

Thus it is not uncommon to find that when a large-scale evangelistic project is mounted in some area, it numbers among its detractors Christians of a differing viewpoint.

In practice, most organised evangelism in Britain is carried out by those of the evangelical tradition, and because we represent a minority within the Church at large, the credibility and effectiveness of what we are doing is impaired.

What then is the Christian scenario in the United Kingdom today? In what follows I shall major on the English situation which I know best.

If the first fact of life which I have to face is that I belong to a minority within a minority, the second is that the Christian minority is a shrinking one. I have heard differing estimates as to when the rot set in, but most observers would agree that the churches have been in numerical decline since the First World War at least.

The decline is more marked in relation to membership as opposed to attendance. It is not uncommon to find churches that have higher attendances than their official membership figures would suggest. My own denomination, the Church of England, is declining at a rate of 2.6 per cent per annum, according to the *U.K. Christian Handbook*. We are now confirming roughly half the number we confirmed twenty-five years ago.

It is inevitable that when decline has been a fact of life for several decades, a certain defeatism creeps into one's attitudes and future planning. Perhaps the word 'defeatism' should not be used, but I cannot think of a more precise description. The 1983 Tiller Report attempted to set out a strategy for the deployment of the clergy for the years to come, and it based its arguments on the assumption that there was little ground for believing that the Church of England could ever raise the number of full-time clergy that traditional approaches to staffing would demand.

This numerical decline, with all the attendant evidences of closed churches and chapels from place to place, only reinforces the assumption that is held by many people, that Christianity is a spent force and that we live in an increasingly secular society.

American socioligist Peter Berger has suggested that when

the churches are in this sort of situation they find themselves in the middle of a 'deadly dilemma':

> They can either accommodate themselves to the situation, play the pluralistic game of religious free enterprise, and come to terms as best they can with the plausibility problem by modifying their product in accordance with consumer demands. Or they can refuse to accommodate themselves, entrench themselves behind whatever socio-religious structures they can maintain or construct, and continue to profess the old objectives as much as possible as if nothing had happened (*The Sacred Canopy*, 1969).

Those two key words 'accommodation' and 'entrenchment' provide the clues to understanding what I see in the churches and Christian traditions of my country. And both the Christianity of accommodation and the Christianity of entrenchment are harmful to the cause of evangelism.

When describing traditions within Christianity, labels fly thick and fast: 'Catholic', 'evangelical', 'liberal', 'radical', 'modernist', 'fundamentalist', 'Protestant', and so one can go on. Most denominations are coalitions of two or three of these strands and some of the strands come together so that you can have 'liberal Catholics' and 'liberal Protestants' – the permutations are almost endless! People grouped under these various labels insist that the differences are to do with theology, but I have a sneaking suspicion that Peter Berger is nearer the truth in most cases. It is true that the basic Catholic/Protestant division is historical and theological, but I suggest that the whole liberal modernist, radical versus conservative elements are really reflections of this 'deadly dilemma' which Berger has identified.

In 1984 Professor David Jenkins was called from his academic work to become Bishop of Durham. A warm-hearted, slightly impish intellectual, he was soon in deep trouble as a result of his comments in television interviews. As he answered questions it became clear that he very much doubted that Jesus was born of a virgin. He believed God was capable of doing such a thing, but saw no reason why he needed to. Again, when it came to the Resurrection of Christ he argued that what such a belief entailed was far more than 'a conjuring trick with bones'. There was, he argued, by the very nature of historical research, no way we could be sure of the empty tomb and 'no certainty about anything in the New Testament'.

These statements sent shock waves through the churches, and strong pressure was brought to bear on the Archbishop of York to cancel or postpone the consecration.

In fact, Dr Jenkins was only saying the sort of thing that 'liberal' Christians have been saying for years. And behind it all is a tradition within which, for the best possible reason (the preservation of a credible faith in an increasingly sceptical world), one accommodates to the way the world seems to think. Thus someone who thinks as Dr Jenkins does can say to a sceptic, 'No – we are not saying that the body of Jesus was "magicked" out of the tomb. For all we know the bones may still be lying around somewhere. What we are saying is that after Christ's death his disciples became increasingly aware that he and all he stood for was still alive. The last word about Jesus is not death but risenness!'

My feeling about all this is that the sorts of people I meet who are supposed to be impressed by this sort of accommodation are more likely to brand such thinking as a 'cop out'.

In his book *The Church of England – Where is it Going?* David Holloway, the vicar of a large and growing church in Newcastle, took Dr Jenkins and his arguments to task. He argued strongly for the plain meaning of such phrases as 'virgin birth' and 'bodily resurrection'.

Holloway's book occasioned a remarkable open letter in the *Church Times* from David Edwards, the erudite provost of

Southwark. The words of that open letter are to me the most eloquent defence of accommodationist thinking I have read. The crux of Edwards's defence of Dr Jenkins' right to be a bishop and to hold the views that he does, lies in these words:

> But are these 'doubting bishops' utterly wrong to be open to hesitations about the nature or extent of the miraculous? Most of the British do have such doubts nowadays, when the doubts have not developed into outright denials. Must every bishop be as you are, immune to doubt? And, if so, why stop at bishops? Must every clergyman be as you are? Must everyone be truly entitled to be a Christian?
>
> ... I gain the impression that it does not fill you with amazement that a baby boy should be born to a mother who has never 'known' a man; and that a corpse should be transformed into a body able to walk among disciples without being recognised, and to pass through doors ...
>
> I hope you will not be personally offended if I call you innocent. In the days before science and scientific history almost all religious people were innocent in this field ...
>
> ... I have to protest that you are restricting evangelism to people with minds as innocent as your own or to people who have decided, after wrestling with the problem, that miracles do happen. Surely it is not impossible for the essential gospel to be communicated to *and received by* people who, rightly or wrongly, can no more believe in this sort of miracle than black people can become white?

From the standpoint of an evangelist longing to see the spread of the Gospel in Britain, I find David Edwards's words moving. They show his understanding of the sincerity of intent that lies behind a great deal of accommodationist thinking. To brand such people as traitors to the faith is to be grossly unfair. Those of us who are conservative in our

All One Body? 41

thinking are often guilty of a contempt for 'liberals' and the like.

However, as David Edwards wants to make his case from the standpoint of evangelism, I feel I must try to reply from the same standpoint. I think the accommodationist position which he is defending (he himself is more 'conservative' than Jenkins in my judgment) is misguided because it seems to be saying that making a sale is more important than the nature of the product being sold.

The argument seems to run thus. We have a product that contains the miraculous. Our potential customers cannot easily accept the existence of the miraculous. We must change the product so that it no longer contains this miraculous element. In Peter Berger's words we are 'modifying the product in accordance with consumer demand.'

It seems to my simple mind that there is a dishonesty here. The important question is, surely, what is *the truth about the product*? If the truth is that the product does indeed contain the miraculous, then faced with a market which has difficulties in accepting the miraculous we have a harder selling job! When St Paul went to Athens with the message of the resurrection, he was laughed out of court. It did not, I note, cause him to change what he had to say.

I am typing this chapter on an electronic typewriter which makes use of a 'daisy-wheel'. I have had this device, and the way it works, explained to me. I must honestly say that I find it hard to believe that it does what it does. Surely if one is typing at a rate of up to sixty words a minute this wheel with letters round its circumference cannot possibly be whirling round and selecting each letter in the microseconds available for such an operation.

If I hadn't used this machine or heard about daisy-wheels, and a typewriter salesman tried to explain it to me I think I might even have thought he was pulling my leg! So what should the salesman do? Should he take the daisy-wheel out and sell it to me in a condition where it will not type at all?

No. I suggest he has two options open to him. The first is to try to open up my understanding into new areas. And the second is to give me a demonstration of the machine, showing that it really does work and that, whether I find it easy to believe or not, the only device in the machine which implants the type on the paper is this amazing little daisy-wheel!

My plea to the accommodationist is that the truth about the Gospel does not allow the filtering out of elements which any particular mind-set finds difficult. The evangelist has a higher responsibility than that of making converts. He or she is meant to tell the truth, even, as we frequently see in the New Testament, if it leads to rejection.

In practice I find the issue is not quite so black and white as this and perhaps there is more common ground with the views of David Edwards than at first appears. There are many people who are like the man who said to Jesus, 'I do believe; help me overcome my unbelief!' (Mark 9:24). The evangelist is not setting a doctrine examination before his potential converts. He is saying, 'Taste and see! Bring your doubts. Take what step of faith you can at this moment and be ready for more!'

I believe in daisy-wheels! I have seen others using them. I have used one myself. I still don't *understand* how they work!

The majority of British Christians are within traditions that are trying to accommodate to the secular mind – set in one way or another. I think it has to be said also that it is these accommodationist groupings who are showing the most rapid numerical decline.

Among the conservative groupings, however, there are many churches showing numerical growth. The most striking phenomenon on the British Christian scene is the growth of what has been called the House Church movement. This network of loosely linked, independent congregations is determined not only to hold on to the beliefs that the New Testament writers proclaimed, but also attempts to 'restore' the very structures that they believe can be discerned in those writings. One current estimate of their rate of growth is 30 per cent per annum.

So is everything in the conservative garden lovely and beneficial to the cause of evangelism? Far from it. Peter Berger's term 'entrenchment' is all too uncomfortably accurate. The whole point of a trench is that of protection. Conservative evangelicalism (and this, remember, is the tradition that is most convinced about the priority of evangelism) usually manages to organise itself so that the world is kept well out of sight.

There are several ways this can be done. An extreme example is to act on the text '. . . come out from them and be separate' (2 Cor. 6:17). The Exclusive Brethren used to base their isolationist strategy on this and there are some extreme fellowships within the House Church movement where similar isolationism exists.

But there is more than one way for a group so to entrench itself that its members never mix with those outside. If a group totally organises itself so that there is no time left for its members to spend free time in the presence of unbelievers, it may say that it is not an exclusive fellowship, but in practice it is precisely that. This is, I suggest, the dominating tendency affecting evangelical and charismatic Christianity in Britain.

The lively evangelical church spawns an astonishing number of activities for its members. There are prayer-groups, Bible studies, committees plus the running of organisations for youth and children (which, admittedly, can be bridging operations into the community at large).

If our lively evangelical congregation belongs to a denomination then there may well be calls on some of the key members to play their part in the affairs of the church. Even here we have not painted the full picture.

Evangelical Christianity has become a totally enclosed way of life. The evangelical community has its own, highly competitive publishing industry. Every year scores of new titles are published and several publishing companies are constantly searching for material to meet the great demands that they have, themselves, helped to create. The same applies to records. The community has its own recording stars who take part in concert tours and large rallies throughout the country. Evangelical films (mostly imported from the USA) have been with us for decades and now there is the logical move into the field of video.

But there is more! The evangelical community has also a booming holiday industry. Evangelical magazine pages are full of advertisements for Christian guest-houses, Christian tours, be it to the Holy Land or the ski slopes, and now the latest phenomenon is the giant county showground holiday convention with thousands of people coming together in their tents and caravans to have a mixture of holiday and Bible convention.

My problem with all this is that there is no element within the mix of which I disapprove. Why shouldn't we publish? Why shouldn't those Christians who may belong to tiny, struggling fellowships have the inspiration of joining with scores, hundreds, even thousands of others for a holiday plus the chance to experience the ministry of gifted Bible teachers?

Again, in the whole field of Christian education, why shouldn't we produce films, videos, tapes and other resource materials to help Christians learn about their Lord and their calling to worship and to witness?

Every individual element can be justified, but the end-product of all the elements together can often be people who are totally shielded from the world and totally insensitive to the way the very people they want to see converted actually live and move and have their being. *One of the most vivid discoveries I made while working with the Mission England project was not the alienation of the world from the Church, but the alienation of so many churches and Christians from the world.*

This unwitting alienation showed itself particularly in an insensitivity. Evangelism has to be thought out from the potential convert backwards at least as much as from the desire to preach forwards. I kept finding an inability to do this.

For example, posters for some evangelistic activity would be worded more with a view to being approved of by the insider than to being understood by (let alone appealing to) the outsider. I can think of a special service in a church which I attended which was billed as a 'guest service'. Members of the church had no doubt been told to bring their unconverted friends. Once inside the building (if they ever got that far) not one concession was made to help such people feel at home. The service was devoid of any familiar hymns – everything musical was contemporary praise material. This posed two problems. First, only the keen insiders knew it. Second, the singer was called upon to sing explicitly about his or her own adoration for the very God whose existence he or she doubted.

This insensitivity to the realities of the wider world shows itself in many other ways. Evangelistic systems are evolved that seem persuasive to the insider, but, frankly, make no impression whatsoever even on those outside who are seeking. Assumptions are made concerning the starting-points for a conversation about Christ which when put to the test prove to be too far along the line to be of help.

Speakers of note pontificate about the 'problems' that are affecting the world. The faithful hang on every word and feel reassured that they know the answer to their neighbour's problems only to find that their neighbour seems as happy as a sand-boy and has few worries other than the price of beer. It was Bishop David Sheppard some years ago who said that the big problem facing the Church was not the miserable sinner but the happy pagan!

This entrenched mentality often leads to an inordinate admiration of evangelists. They are the heroic figures who go out and win the lost, while the rest seem less successful – usually because they have too little time or too little contact. The truth all too often (as I intend to explain more fully later) is that the evangelists have to go where they are wanted and all too often the places where they are wanted are the places where their particular gifts are hardly needed. They go through the motions of preaching to the lost in front of congregations that are well and truly saved; no one comes forward, and very subtly many of those who most believe in evangelism also believe that it doesn't work any more.

Eddie Gibbs used to say that many pastors invite an evangelist to come to their churches half hoping for the comforting experience of seeing them fail also!

Jesus clearly saw the danger of this sort of thing happening. Why else did he refer to lights being put under a bowl or salt losing its saltiness?

It would, however, be totally unfair to give the impression that evangelical Christians are complacent about these introverting tendencies. There are many pastors and church leaders who are trying to turn their congregations inside out, and there is a growing number of cases where progress is being made. Their task, however, is not made easier by the increasing effects of commercial pressures. Publishers are in constant need of finding something *new*. If people are to keep coming into the Christian bookshops to buy new books, then there must be the promise of something new to draw them in. This has led to fashions and fads and the throwing-up of new teachers and writers with some new emphasis. This in turn is reflected on the platforms of the growing number of holiday conventions, and it isn't long before the new emphasis is being described as 'what the Spirit is now saying to the churches!'

The local pastor all too often has a cruel choice. Either he has to spend time countering what he may feel is an undesirable slant or he has to run with it himself, thereby giving the emphasis more credence and also making himself one of 'yesterday's men' when eventually a new emphasis breaks through and takes centre stage. In no area is this following the fashion dynamic more evident than in those churches most affected by the charismatic renewal. And the tragedy here is that they often have so much to offer if only they could spare the time from their collective obsession to be following the latest new thing.

I do not enjoy saying this. I am all too aware that I myself could be going in the opposite direction and hardening my heart against new insights that really are from God. For me the acid test is this. Do these new teachings improve the effectiveness of the witness as well as the worship of the churches involved? When one hears of cases of churches caught up in fashion-following spirituality which have grown, all too often closer analysis reveals that the growth has taken place because of existing Christians transferring-in rather than new Christians being 'made' from among those who previously did not believe. The congregation in question becomes for a while a centre of spiritual excitement and draws to itself those who have an appetite for that sort of thing. This accounts for the remarkable growth of some (by no means all) of the House Churches. What encourages me, however, is that a growing number of House-Church leaders are seeing this for themselves and giving a strong lead to their congregations to turn outwards in evangelism.

If the House Churches have been among the most clearly entrenched and fashion-following of Britain's Christian communities, I believe the next ten years could show them to be the most effective and courageous witnesses to the community at large. Their discipline, commitment and trust in the supernatural are an example to all of us who name the name of Christ. Time alone will tell.

Overall, however, the present situation affecting the evangelical and charismatic Christian scene is marked by strong traces of spiritual self-indulgence and alienation from the world in which most people live.

As we tried to set up Mission England and to unite as many churches as possible behind a single nationwide Gospel outreach we found ourselves staring at a dilemma. If we majored on the accommodationists, they were the ones with most contacts in the world at large, but often most anxieties about the sort of message associated with Billy Graham. If we limited ourselves to those who would sign a basis of faith pleasing to the more entrenched conservative evangelicals, we stood the chance of reaching far fewer unconverted people! What has to be seen clearly in any set-piece evangelistic project is that, big or small, the only sure way of guaranteeing non-Christian attendance is through the Christian friends such people may have.

What we tried to do was to put our plans on the table in the view of all and say frankly that we had no intention of losing control of the project or changing the theological assumptions. Having said that, we would also say, 'If you want to come and join us, then whatever may be your position you were welcome as an equal.' (Obviously, heretical, non-Trinitarian groups would have had to be excluded, but in practice the problem hardly arose.)

This sounds all well and good, but it isn't as simple as it appears and we soon found ourselves walking on perilous tight-ropes. There are few conservative Christians who would want to discourage 'liberal' Christians from praying and bringing people along to evangelistic meetings. The problem for them arises if people such churches have brought along profess conversion. Should they be encouraged to go back?

It is at this point that I see the full force of the conservative fear. Suppose someone has responded to Billy Graham (or any evangelist). That person has heard a statement of Christianity that takes the Resurrection at face value, that holds the Bible to be 'the Word of God' that calls for a certain type of discipleship. What happens when such people are referred back to a church where the minister believes the Resurrection accounts are a poetic expression rather than a description of historical effects, who considers the Bible to be full of errors, who is embarrassed by extempore prayer and does not expect prayers to be capable of changing anything?

To send a new Christian, full of new enthusiasms and new certainties back to receive such treatment is to run the risk of doing untold emotional and spiritual harm. This problem showed up in an extreme form with regard to those who claimed an allegiance to the Roman Catholic church. Some priests were totally opposed to what we were doing and were likely to greet converts with a rebuke, while a growing number of priests were likely to be fully in support and seemed almost more evangelical than evangelicals! It was with Roman and Anglo-Catholics that I saw the very best effects of the charismatic movement.

One area within one of our Mission England regions was brought to life through the prayers and endeavours of a Roman Catholic family. They organised prayer support and put together a committee. Then with a selfless wisdom that still brings a lump to my throat, they persuaded a local Protestant to be the chairman so as to avoid giving offence to evangelicals in the region at large. They shall have their reward . . .

Our answer to the problem was to say that enquirers without church links would only be sent to churches that were on record as having sent people to train to lead six-week nurture groups. If a church brought a party to the meetings and if some in that church party went forward for counselling, and if that church was not on record as having nurture-group facilities, then while we did not redirect the enquirers, we did try to attach them to an independent neighbourhood nurture group at the same time.

In this way we tried to guarantee that a 'new Christian' would receive initial support and Christian teaching that was in keeping with the message to which they had responded in the first place. It was not a perfect answer, but we were convinced that a perfect answer did not exist. We knew from past experience that forcible attempts to redirect people who already had a church affiliation rarely succeed and not only antagonise the church that was spurned but can also disillusion the 'new Christian'.

I cannot pretend, however, that the system worked perfectly. It didn't, and in many cases attempts to set up these neighbourhood nurture groups failed. In other cases, especially in urban situations, 'working-class' people found attendance at nurture groups too threatening and a reminder of being 'back at school'.

It would be wrong, however, to close this chapter at this point. Almost all that I have set out has been problem-orientated. There are enough signs of change, enough blowings of new winds to prove to me that God's Spirit is on the move. Mission England was full of surprises as well as disappointments and frustrations. In East Anglia the enthusiastic support of Bishops Maurice Wood of Norwich and John Wain of St Edmondsbury and Ipswich led to a significant number of churches that would not be labelled 'conservative' or 'evangelical' taking part. Barriers came down and people listened to each other and put aside their prejudices. A similar story could be told about churches in the South-West. In Liverpool what was nearly an explosive

All One Body?

situation concerning the high degree of interest from the Roman Catholics was eased by very gracious moves of the hierarchy, who recognised the almost impossible situation in which our local organisers were placed over balancing traditional Protestant fears and suspicions against the strong Roman Catholic desire to play their part fully.

When we went into the Mission England enterprise I expected a theological backlash from churches and church leaders who took a more liberal or accommodationist stance. That backlash did not come. Our main opponents – and fierce they often were – came from the ultra-conservative Protestants. They picketed and occasionally disrupted our meetings and I was continually hearing of tapes that were being circulated in independent churches attacking us for identifying with liberals and ecumenists and Roman Catholics.

I have come to the conclusion that many non-evangelical Christian leaders deliberately decided to give us an easy ride. It was difficult not to feel that many who could not easily agree with us theologically were saying, 'God bless you, we also want to see Mission England succeed.' There is a growing awareness that Britain is in desperate need of a spiritual renewal and anything that sets out to glorify God and call men to consider Christ is worthy of respect if not whole-hearted support.

Christians in Britain are a minority group full of inner dividing lines. I'm sure Satan likes it that way. Some of us, from good motives as well as bad, have tried to accommodate to the mind-set and assumptions of our times. Others from equally good and bad motives have created a nearly self-contained pious world in which to live and feel unpressurised by the immensity of the unbelieving world 'out there'.

I believe we need to see why each of us has done what we have done, or to be more accurate, has inherited what we have inherited. Few of us have actually looked up a *Which* magazine on Christian traditions and gone for the best buy. Christianity has not come to us in a vacuum. It has come to us enshrined in a tradition. We have, as Christians, responded to the only Christ that was on offer in our personal circumstances. I am an evangelical because it was an evangelical church that reached out and gathered me in as a boy who was already open to Christ because of my parents' way of life. Humanly speaking, it could as easily have been an accommodationist church. That does not mean that I abandon my conviction that (in spite of these human and accidental factors) evangelicalism is in fact the most correct expression of the Christian faith. What it should mean is that I respect the liberal Christian who may have a similar conviction about the correctness of his or her position. I must respect such a person's sincerity, and I must recognise that he or she has said the same 'yes' as I have, to the only Christ with which they were presented.

I have to recognise also that peer pressures being what they are, Christian traditions tend to breed true and to reinforce themselves. Confrontation and polemic will not change the situation. It only puts us into defensive postures. Only love and dialogue and the deepest respect will change things. It is the way I have tried to follow in recent years and particularly as I tried to lead Mission England.

It isn't always easy!

4

Did Mission England Succeed?

I was invited to a meeting of a subcommittee of the British Council of Churches Standing Committee for Evangelism. (That's a mouthful!)

As I arrived at the meeting, I was given the inevitable cup of coffee and began to recognise familiar faces around the table. The chairman opened up the discussion with the words, 'Well, Gavin, you've certainly proved that there is still a place for crusade evangelism in Britain!'

It was indeed gratifying to be told this, especially by the sort of person who does not lightly jump on to bandwagons. My reply was to say that I felt it was important to see Mission England as something far more than traditional crusade evangelism, and that I should be dismayed if enthusiasts thought that all they had to do was to set up big meetings with big-name speakers.

Was Mission England a success? The only correct answer to this is to say that we must wait and see. However, there is value in studying what the project set out to do and measuring what happened against its basic aims.

Very early in the setting-up process, Tom Houston, then executive director of the Bible Society, accepted the role of chairman and formulated a statement of objective which read as follows:

> To provide opportunities for a large number of people in five regions to hear and respond to the Gospel of Jesus Christ before, during and after a series of mass meetings to be addressed by Dr Billy Graham, by motivating and training Christians and local churches to share the Gospel with their friends and contacts and welcome those who respond into the on-going life of the churches.

From this statement several things can be seen which show that we were thinking of something far more than a 'crusade' and that we were trying to cope with some of the problems I have been outlining in the previous chapters.

We were thinking of a timescale of about three years. We were concentrating our efforts within clearly defined regions. We were starting from the concern to motivate and train Christians and local churches. We were clear that the key element was to do with the contacts and friends of existing Christians. We were looking to Billy Graham's 'mass-meeting' ministry not only to be effective in itself, but to act as a catalyst to make these other things happen. Finally we were aware that particular attention was needed with regard to integrating and 'welcoming' those who respond into the on-going life of the churches.

As I began to travel round the country sharing the vision of Mission England I found the management-style compressed wording of our master objective needed to be put in another way. British Christians do not easily respond to the notion of having objectives and being business-like! It is one of our great failings. We readily complain if our vicar or pastor is inefficient, but get extremely uneasy if he starts talking in terms of efficiency, management, objective-setting and the like! I sometimes think that the Church of England is the last stronghold of the amateur captain now that cricket has gone the way of all flesh!

Did Mission England Succeed?

I preferred to set out four broad aims for Mission England.
1. To glorify God.
2. To alert the nation to the importance of spiritual issues.
3. To motivate local churches to do their own evangelism.
4. To bring a large number of people to personal faith in Christ.

I thought it was important to start with the reminder that nothing is more important than the glory of God. This acted as a constant reminder to us on the staff that our means had to be as worthy as our ends. It soon became clear to me that I was up to my eyes in ecclesiastical politics. We were quickly in the position where we could play one group off against another and where we could tactically conceal things rather than be totally open at all times.

I remember talking over such matters with Brian Mills as we drove home together from yet another committee meeting. Brian had been seconded from the Evangelical Alliance to be my assistant national director and is one of the most prayerful and spiritual men I know. Together we agreed that we must try to 'walk in the light' in all our leadership. That if we were vulnerable we should never try to hide the fact and if we were in positions of power we should never try to exploit the fact.

I'm sure we did not always succeed, but it was the right thing to aim at.

A concern for the glory of God meant that we had to rely on him rather than on our great plans and organisations. Brian set out to make prayer the first priority in the project. His aim was to give it a high profile and never to let any of us, at any level of operation, forget that prayer came first.

His greatest contribution was the 'Prayer Triplets' idea. Like all brilliant ideas it was simple! Three people meet regularly to pray. Each person shares with the others the names of three people known to him or her who do not as yet believe in Christ. Thus the prayer-group of three prays for nine and each member is encouraged in his/her day-by-day relations with the people being prayed for. We started the scheme nearly two years before Billy Graham preached his first sermon in Bristol and long before he arrived we were hearing of delighted Christians telling us of answers to their prayers.

My hope was also that the very size of the Mission England project would help us to break out of the closed Christian world and into public awareness. In this regard there is no doubt that Billy Graham himself was our trump-card. Wherever he went we had intensive press, radio and television attention. When the 1984 series of meetings was over we literally measured the media attention that he had been given. The national press had published 157 items and eleven editorials covering nearly 3,000 column inches. The regional press (and we were deliberately working to capitalise on regional awareness) published 1,262 items plus eighteen editorials taking up no less than 37,116 column inches!

Radio time amounted to nearly eight and a half hours and television time amounted to five hours seven minutes. Just short of 10,000 letters were received as a result of the broadcasts, mostly asking for counselling material.

All this was on top of the total attendance figures at the stadium meetings which were 1,026,600 with an estimated further attendance of 200,000 at meetings using video-tapes made at the stadiums and rushed to venues around the country by Datapost. Possibly another 100,000 people attended meetings addressed by the associate evangelists (mostly British) who worked alongside Dr Graham.

An extensive advertising campaign was run in the regions and also in the regional and national press. Millions of homes were visited with literature commending the meetings and linked to the organisation of bus parties from local churches.

Did Mission England Succeed?

I have no doubt that the public awareness about spiritual issues was significantly raised – at least in the regions involved. We commissioned Gallup polls to survey the public awareness in Bristol, Sunderland and Merseyside. We found that 93 per cent of the public in Bristol were aware that Billy Graham was about to speak at a series of meetings. The pollsters assured us that they had never encountered such high 'product awareness'. In Sunderland and Liverpool the figures were 84 and 87 per cent respectively.

This may seem a far cry from awareness about spiritual issues, but it was not. The name Billy Graham was clearly linked to the Christian agenda as other questions asked by Gallup soon revealed. From all sides both with regard to the 1984 meetings and also in 1985 in Sheffield when Billy Graham returned for a further series, the reports poured in that Christianity was being talked about in the shops, on the buses, in the pubs and at work. Some may object that it was less than the best for the subject to have to be attached to a high-profile personality, but the truth of the matter is that life is like that. I'm quite sure that the eccentricities of John the Baptist helped forward religious discussions in his day! God has always used personalities – after all, he was the one who created the personalities in the first place.

The third main objective was that evangelism might be stimulated in and through the churches themselves. Before I consider this any further it is worth noting that some 6,000 separate churches became involved in the project. There is no doubt in my mind that the extent of commitment varied greatly from church to church. For some the only level of involvement was the preparation for and support of the main meetings in the football grounds. But even if no more than that was done, a great many useful things were taken on board. Prayer was stimulated. The Christian life and witness classes gave people a vision and some skills to share the Gospel and to know how to deal with some basic types of spiritual enquiry. The Operation Andrew concept of people strengthening their friendships with the unconverted and asking them to come to the meetings could not but push the boundaries out and create some good habits. Nurture-group training and the creation of sensitivity towards the awkwardness many feel at coming into a church congregation was certainly something of lasting benefit and I keep hearing of churches that now have nurture groups as part of their continuing strategy.

All these things were surely valuable helps to local church evangelism plus one other vital if intangible contribution. The Mission England project did something for the morale of many congregations – not least those that are small and struggling.

The morale factor greatly affects evangelism. With Christians so often reminded that they are in a minority, and a minority that is fast losing the influence that it used to have, it was exhilarating to be involved in something so big that many outsiders were forced to sit up and take notice. Even the prophet Elijah needed the encouragement of being told that there were 7,000 others in Israel whose knees had not bowed to Baal.

The Mission England meetings encouraged many to believe again that people *do* get converted – even today! There are still many churches which have not seen a convert in recent years, and many ministers who do not quite know what to do when they are faced with such a person.

For those churches who entered more fully into the three-year period of emphasis which the project was trying to create, there was more to receive. In 1983, a year before the main meetings, we held ministers' seminars on local-church evangelism at many points around the country. Alas, some of them were poorly supported, which was partly due to the poor state of our communications at that time in some regions. Where they were successful, vision and skills were

Did Mission England Succeed?

imparted to ministers in such areas of evangelism as visiting, small groups, guest services and evangelistic preaching and so on. It is impossible to measure how much home-brewed evangelism was generated through these seminars as well as through ideas circulated in the 'leadership' bulletin but I know of specific cases where churches took new initiatives and began to discover for themselves that people can indeed be brought to faith in Christ.

One of the things that I have always been clear about is that unless evangelism is put firmly on the local church's agenda – and this usually requires a concrete proposal – it tends to get crowded out of congregational life. Thanks to the prospect of Billy Graham's large-scale meetings, Mission England was able to set and even dominate the agenda in hundreds of churches over a period of two or three years.

We learnt from past failures. We knew that if we tried to devise timetables and call all of our churches to be doing this or that all at the same time we should end up playing games and being ignored, to say nothing of creating guilt feelings all round. Our approach was to give a vision, show up some of the elements in the vision, describe possible options and provide resources that matched the options. In 1982 we produced (with the expert help of the Scripture Union) an excellent group-study book entitled *Care to Say Something*. This tried to help entrenched-mentality Christians to be sensitive to where people really are and to see that witnessing was something far more than having a few catch-phrases to use at appropriate times. Our vision was to help people to become integrated as conversationalists so that their faith could be more naturally expressed in the discussion topics that more usually crop up in everyday situations. It is very rare for someone to be asked, 'What must I do to be saved?'

This resource book matched up with the vision we were trying to share in 1982 of Christians taking positive steps in life to be more outgoing – coming out of the trenches. I remember developing a line of patter: 'Where do you think converts come from? Do they grow on trees? Do you think evangelists bring them with them in a tin – just add water? No, they come from the friends and contacts of existing Christians or they don't come at all!'

The prayer triplets scheme was also part of this whole attempt to make Christians turn outwards. In recent years I have noted that churches tend to pray more and more for themselves and that when prayer ever turns outwards it so often becomes generalised and imprecise. Brian Mills tried to get these small groups to pray specifically for those outside the 'fold'. One by-product of this scheme was that it often rekindled intercessory prayer in local church life. One East Anglian pastor claimed that prayer triplets had created a prayer-meeting in a church which had never had one before. A Bristol minister of a small Baptist congregation said to me in 1983, 'I have a congregation of eighty and already sixty are in prayer triplets.'

What in effect happened was that churches rarely took up all the options but many took up most. We shall never know how many people were won to faith in Christ before Dr Graham arrived in May 1984, but I believe the number is not small. I remember speaking at a retreat organised in Lancaster University in April 1984. During a break between sessions two or three young people came up to me in a group and one spoke on behalf of the others. 'We wanted to say that we count it a privilege to have been converted during Mission England.'

Anthony Bush, who directed our activities in the South-West, told me several times that he was convinced that more people would be won to Christ in the third year of the project than in the middle year which included the successful Ashton Gate meetings in Bristol. Certainly we discovered that the nurture groups became evangelistic as many of the new Christians brought along friends and relatives. One church

Did Mission England Succeed?

in Anthony's region reported fourteen conversions through their nurture groups set up after the stadium meetings.

I dare to believe that many churches were revived and helped to become evangelising congregations as a result of what we were doing. One bishop wrote to us after we had circulated some statistics:

> There is, I think, a hidden aspect of Mission England which statistics do not reveal. There is a sense in which the impact has been much wider and deeper than is generally realised, and is to some extent actually masked by the publication of head counts. As I travel round the Diocese a year after the Mission, I find parishes which have been greatly influenced by the experience, but not in ways one can analyse statistically. I mean that for parishes of all ecclesiastical traditions, outreach has become much more central to their life as well as the nurture of Christians new and old.

I have heard similar comments from other Anglican bishops and from some key Methodists also.

The fourth of the broad aims that I kept before me has, to some extent, already been answered. We wanted, please God, 'to bring a large number of people to personal faith in Christ.' The immediately available statistics from the meetings were impressive. No less than 96,982 enquirers came forward during the 1984 meetings and a further 26,131 decisions were registered at Sheffield a year later. In addition to the meetings in Sheffield, we also transmitted five of the meetings live via satellite to fifty-one other venues in the British Isles drawing an attendance of 181,356 with the result that a further 8,186 people sought counselling.

In 1984, in addition to the main meetings, we had just over 180 video missions around the country. Local committees prepared along similar lines as for the large stadium missions. For four successive nights they would show video recordings of one of the Billy Graham meetings that had taken place earlier that same week – sometimes the live and the video meeting were only twenty-four hours apart. It is hard to be precise, but we have reason to believe that these video missions drew in a further 200,000 people with an estimated response of around 4,000 seeking counsel.

There is little doubt in my mind that the United Kingdom has never seen anything like this in its history. However, it is one thing for someone to get up and go forward at an evangelistic meeting, it is quite another to claim that such a person is invariably a 'convert'. Those who went forward at our meetings fell into several categories.

In the 1984 meetings 56 per cent of all who went forward were 'accepting Christ' for the first time. They were stating that they held no faith and no committment before that moment. In Sheffield the following year the proportion had risen to 63 per cent. The two other categories of response were, 'assurance' and 'rededication', and an assortment of responses that don't fit under either of these heads is simply categorised as 'other'.

So it is that about 60 per cent of the gross figure represents what could well turn out to be 'conversions'. Even then, however, we cannot simply assume that such a figure represents the final figure. There is a fall-away factor. In the Parable of the Sower Jesus (Luke 8:1–15) talked about the seed that fell on rocky ground which sprouted quickly but died from lack of soil depth, and also the seed among thorn bushes which choked the life out of the growing plants. The parable was about people and their responses to God and it has, alas, always proved accurate. There were those who fell away and it is difficult to know the statistics for such a figure.

In the South-West we conducted a poll from churches in the region to which referrals had been made. The poll was

Did Mission England Succeed?

conducted twelve months after the Bristol meetings and replies were received from 174 churches. The replies to the questionnaire revealed that after six months 70 per cent of all referred back to the churches were still in contact. After twelve months that figure had dropped to 59 per cent. (The figure was made up from 52 per cent still in contact with the church to which they had first been referred plus a further 7 per cent who had moved on and linked with another church after moving house.)

These figures are very encouraging, but it needs to be borne in mind that referrals to churches covered *all* sorts of responses and not only the first-time 'acceptances'. What we don't know from these statistics is whether the category most affected by the fall away was the 'acceptance' category.

There were particular fall-away problems with churches close to the actual stadiums where the meetings were held. They were the churches which had the highest percentage of totally unattached people who had drifted in to hear the preacher without the benefit of being accompanied by a Christian friend. It was often difficult to make further progress with them and the strategy of a nurture group didn't always work with these sorts of people.

All this bore out what we had suspected. 'Crusade' evangelism has to go hand in hand with parallel activity at the personal level. The big evangelistic meeting is not a replacement for personal faith sharing, it is a resource. Billy Graham had always stressed this when he talked of his enthusiasm for the Operation Andrew programme. He knows that the secret of an effective evangelistic meeting is praying Christians bringing along the people they are praying for. Where the churches don't have pre-crusade links with the enquirer, the task of holding on to them afterwards is very difficult. I remember hearing of a survey carried out in the United States which revealed that the biggest factor affecting whether a person will join a congregation following an evangelistic meeting is whether that person has personal friends in the congregation.

We have already noted that the nurture groups and other forms of local-church activity seemed, at least in some places, to carry on the evangelising momentum of the main meetings. The survey of 174 churches in the South-West a year after the Bristol meetings revealed that between them they could account for a further 976 individuals who could be classed as 'new Christians' or converts *since* those meetings had taken place.

So can we say that Mission England has been a success? The answer must be that it is still too early to be sure. There is, however, a great deal of evidence that suggests that considerable progress was made in the pursuit of the four broad aims which I outlined in the early days. We need a few more years to see if there is still evidence that can be measured in such areas as denominational statistics for church attendance and especially in terms of men and women offering for full-time Christian service. The latter factor was most noticeable after the 1954 Harringay crusade.

I believe there is also another factor which by its very nature cannot yet be measured. One of our great hopes for Mission England was that the three-year emphasis on the evangelistic agenda would create evangelising 'habits' which would remain with many churches afterwards and thereby affect church and community for some years to come.

I should dearly love to see this happen, but I have a sinking feeling that many churches will find the pull-back into the old ways almost irresistible. In particular, the fashion-chasing evangelicals and charismatics – who should always be in the forefront of evangelism – are the ones where there is the greatest likelihood of a seduction away from putting evangelism as first priority.

I dare to believe that some lasting – perhaps many lasting

– benefits will have come out of all that we have seen. Again and again in Mission England I got a strange feeling that, for all our organisation, we were not really in charge of what was happening. There was often that sense that a higher authority was making sure that we mortals didn't make too much of a mess of things!

I think that with Mission England we stumbled across a piece of God's agenda. If that is the case, it will have been a success!

5
Learning from Billy

The final meeting of the Greater Sacramento crusade had already started. There had been a choir item and some singing from the 30,000 people gathered on that hot September evening in the fairground race-track.

I had been a guest of the Billy Graham Evangelistic Association and was observing how crusades were conducted. It was 1983, one year before the forty Mission England stadium meetings were due to take place. On that last night of the crusade I was sitting among the counsellors and supervisors next to the platform, facing the great crowd in anticipation of that moment when we expected hundreds to leave their seats and come forward in answer to the evangelists' call to decide for Christ.

On the platform Cliff Barrows, Graham's cheerful and ebullient master of ceremonies had just called us to stand and sing a hymn. I can't remember what it was, but I began to sing along with everyone else around me.

At that moment Billy Graham threaded his way through the temporary stands which housed the choir and began to walk along the line which included me on his way to the platform. A small entourage surrounded him, including the assistant chief of the Sacramento police force who had said to me earlier in the week, 'If someone's going to take a shot at him it won't be in my town!' In an age when people shoot at popes one cannot be too careful.

As I sang away I looked up and caught sight of Billy. We had met twice during the week for discussions. He spotted me and veered over to speak, causing some slight confusion to those minding him. 'Hi, Gavin. I didn't know you were still here. C'mon up on the platform.'

There followed a slightly embarrassing episode, during which an extra seat had to be manhandled up and the local chairman of the crusade was moved sideways from the seat beside where Billy was expected to take his place.

I think I know Billy Graham a little better than I knew him then, but that little episode in California is typical. It is a cameo of the life he lives.

Billy Graham's whole life is built around the thing he does best – speaking about Jesus Christ to large crowds. Billy Graham is never alone. He is always surrounded by minders who see it as their task to smooth the path for him to get from A to B with the minimum of fuss, and to protect him from the veritable army of people who would love to have his undivided attention on matters of relatively little importance. He is so well minded that he often knows little of the secondary matters in which he is necessarily involved.

And behind all the paraphernalia of fame, and all the evidence of high-level organisation and all the power of being able to hold the attention of thousands of people on the subject of Jesus Christ, Billy Graham remains a warm 'country boy', generous and capable on the spur of the moment of making gestures and decisions that do not fit in well with the carefully-prepared plans of his associates.

Billy Graham has two families. There is the family of wife, children and grandchildren ('I'm never quite sure. Ah think we have sixteen of them now'). There is also the other family of his immediate associates whose loyalty to him and to his ministry has to be seen to be believed. Cliff Barrows has worked with Billy since the late 1940s. When Eddie Gibbs, Clive Calver and I spoke with Billy at Nice and we had reached the point in discussion where Billy had said that he would come to England, his first condition was that Cliff Barrows would be working with him. Cliff is far more than a gifted leader of congregational singing and a creator of instant choirs. He is a skilled presenter of programmes, be they from the platform within a packed football stadium or be they from a radio or TV studio. He literally stage-manages an evangelistic meeting so that Billy Graham has nothing to worry about apart from the task of standing up and preaching the Gospel.

Bev Shea, now into his seventies, is a gentle giant of a man still able to sing with a rich, deep, unfaltering tone the old Gospel songs that, apart from anything else, help Billy into the right frame of mind to preach. To watch Shea singing immediately before Billy Graham preaches is to witness a demonstration of self-effacement. There is no attempt to sing for applause — simply to encourage congregational thoughtfulness.

In Britain most of our Gospel singers are performance singers. They sing for applause because the context for their singing is the concert rather than the evangelistic platform. American Gospel singers are mainly of the same sort. They are part of the in-group show-biz of the Christian world. To invite one to sing on an evangelistic platform would not be appropriate unless one was talking in terms of a 'set' of at least fifteen minutes. During the Mission England meetings Bev Shea rarely sang more than one song and in the earlier days with Billy when less use was made of other singers on the nightly programme, Bev would rarely sing more than two songs per meeting.

Seated behind Billy on the platform each night is a boyhood friend: T. W. Wilson, usually known in true 'southern style' as 'TW' or even 'T'. Wilson is Billy's special assistant whose main task is to keep the pressures off his colleague.

Whether it is arranging for laundry, packing suitcases on the last night to allow for a speedy getaway (Graham rarely stays in town after preaching the final sermon of a crusade. Something in his psyche demands that he makes a clean break as quickly as possible), or deciding whether an extra engagement is fitted into the day, TW controls the shots. As with Cliff Barrows, TW is a preacher of proven ability in his own right, but his life is committed to assisting Billy Graham.

All of those close to Billy have made similar sacrifices for him. Dr Walter Smyth, the man directing his international ministry, lives in hotel rooms and jumbo jets for more days in the year than he spends at home in Florida with his wife. Now into his seventies when many would be enjoying retirement, he maintains this globe-trotting life style. Hong Kong, Japan, Australia, Britain, France, and Eastern European capitals are regular pit-stops on an exhausting itinerary and yet he is rarely out of daily contact with his Minneapolis office.

Ask him why he does it and he will give two reasons. First, he believes that Billy Graham is a gift from God to world evangelism. Second, Billy has asked him to carry on.

This same quality pervades the entire Graham organisation. There is no lack of tensions or departmental rivalry. Graham's people are all pretty human and doubtless behave like most people do when caught up in organisational relationships. When one has noted all these common factors, however, there is one overwhelming characteristic they all share and which makes the Billy Graham Evangelistic Association something quite unique. They are all convinced, in a matter-of-fact way, that Billy Graham has a special gift from God and that their job is to see that gift exploited and released to the full.

No father could ever have a more devoted family.

I sometimes wonder how Ruth Graham, wife and mother of five, feels about the other family in Billy's life. They certainly have had the lion's share of her husband's time. It has meant that she has almost single-handedly brought up her children – with results that would make any parents proud.

TW and Cliff once drove me up the mountain byroad to Billy's house in Montreat, North Carolina. Set on top of a hill, it is remote from the rest of the community and offered Ruth the privacy she needed to bring up her children away from the public gaze. While not small, it is no mansion and is simply built from wood with its old rocking-chair on the front porch.

'It's more Ruth's home than Billy's,' said TW's wife. 'Billy's become more used to living in a hotel room!' 'After all those years on the move,' said another in the party, 'I'm not sure he knows how to relax at home any more.'

All of which leads me to register the first lesson that can be learnt from watching Billy – quite simply he's committed. Being an evangelist isn't a job, and in a sense it isn't even a ministry. As far as Billy is concerned it is a compulsion that stems from obedience to his calling. He simply *knows* that he must do it, and go on doing it.

Over the years he has become something of a statesman in the Christian world (and, indeed, in the secular world), but it has never occurred to him that he is meant to graduate out of being a full-time, on-the-road, working evangelist. Billy knows that his preaching days must now be numbered, but that only seems to make him want to get his message over to as many people in as many places as possible.

The day after he landed in England to begin his gruelling 1984 schedule I was due to speak at a training conference in Liverpool. A message was waiting for me when I arrived at the meeting-place. Billy Graham had been admitted to hospital. His voice had been badly affected by a sinus infection for some months and it was clear that we were facing big problems.

A phone call revealed that he was having a minor operation under anaesthetic to use laser techniques to try to clear up the problem. It was obvious that his Sunday evening preaching engagement at Westminster Chapel would have to be cancelled as the operation was due to take place the day before.

On the Saturday I drove back to London as fast as I could to try to pick up the threads. I wanted Billy's busy round of press interviews and television recordings to be cancelled. We were only a week away from the first series of meetings in Bristol. Back home I phoned TW to find out how things were. I was told that Billy still intended to preach at the Westminster Chapel. He would go straight from his hospital bed and return to the same bed after the service!

I shall never forget that service. Billy was clearly weak and a box of large-size tissues was in the pulpit in case he was to have a nose-bleed. At one point in his sermon he raised his arm aloft to make a point, and as the cuff slipped down I could see his plastic, hospital wrist-tag still in place. The voice was barely above a whisper and the thoughts less well held together . . .

But the obedience to a call was there for all to see and as he made his famous call for people to leave their seats and 'accept' Christ, the first fruits of what was to be a record harvest were there for all to see as some 200 people came forward.

I think Billy preached for three reasons that night. The first was because he did not want to let people down. The second was that he did not want to put out a signal about ill health that might damage the chances of full attendances when he went to Bristol. And the third reason was that he sensed that there would be a harvest.

The second basic lesson that I have noted from watching Billy Graham at work is that he is a good learner. There is a genuine humility about him that makes him listen closely to everyone else.

Just before we started the series of meetings in Sheffield in 1985 we held a ministers' meeting. Hundreds of clergy and key lay people were there and the programme was that I was to speak on what we should all be doing when the meetings were over and, after a hymn, Billy would speak.

When I had finished what I had to say, one of Billy's associates said to me, 'You won't be able to give that talk in America – Billy was taking notes!' Sure enough, Billy began his own address by saying that he intended to 'borrow' some of my ideas. It was all very flattering, but I have found that he does this all the time. He has a rapacious appetite for other people's understandings about Christ and Christian ministry. He may not be scholarly in the accepted sense, but he is addicted to listening and learning.

The Sunday before the meetings started at Sheffield he had attended a service at London's famous All Souls Church in Langham Place. Dr John Stott had been preaching on feminism and Billy had been enthralled. He asked for a tape and a transcript. But there was more. What John Stott had said opened up new understandings as far as Billy was concerned, and that meant that one of his proposed sermons (on the family) would have to be changed before he stood up in front of the Sheffield crowd.

I sometimes feel that many of us in Christian ministry have stopped making the effort to stay learners. It is often said that if you study the books on a clergyman's shelves you can see when he stopped reading! Learning is an effort and it is a disturbing activity because it means that one is always having to revise one's assumptions and certainties.

The third lesson that I learned from watching Billy at work was the need for 'professionalism'. This is an area that

Learning from Billy

worries some pious believers. They find it hard to talk in these terms when we are talking about people using Spirit-given gifts and serving the Lord. Shouldn't we just be led by the Lord and avoid relying on human skills?

The answer, I believe, is that part of our obedience to Christ is the application of our minds to the work that we have been given to do and the serious attempt to develop the necessary skills to do the job well.

When we were holding the Mission England meetings in the famous Roker Park stadium in Sunderland, I was sitting on the platform on the evening when BBC Radio were taking most of the meeting live. I knew that the BBC were hoping that Billy would so time things that he gave the invitation at 8.50. I remember thinking that it was asking too much of the man to expect him to preach to an audience of 10,000 people (we were lighter than usual that evening because of the extreme cold and the fact that being a Sunday evening many churches were not sending their usual bus-loads) and at the same time to be fitting in with broadcasting schedules.

As Billy warmed to his subject and developed the theme it became more and more obvious to me that he was not going to be fitting in with the requirements of the BBC.

Built into his lectern there are three lights which are switched on to give a count-down to the appeal on such an occasion. Cliff Barrows controls the switches for these. With ten minutes to go Billy seemed almost in mid-sermon. When the five-minute warning light flashed on I was quite sure that he was ignoring the signal. As the final light came on, or even fractionally before, Billy naturally slipped into the sequence for the invitation. The precision was breathtaking, the more so because it seemed in no way to be forced.

I have watched him preach to three audiences at the same time. There would be the obvious, live congregation packed all around him in the stadium, there would be the live audience gathered in fifty other locations linked by satellite, and there would be the forthcoming television audience watching edited video recordings back in the United States. All three audiences needed different instructions when it came to the manner in which they should express their desire to respond. Billy was able to speak naturally to each at the same time.

I learned later that he finds it a great strain and particularly draining – but none of this is apparent at the time.

The professionalism extends to his attempts to make his preaching relevant. Billy is an avid newspaper reader. He is interested in human affairs in the first place but he also loves to illustrate the points he is making with references to newspaper stories. A colleague, John Wesley White, keeps him well supplied with sheaves of press-cuttings and a skilled researcher-assistant ensures that he is well briefed on just about any matter of national or international significance.

As a result of all this his sermons are in a continual state of revision and he is fiercely self-critical. After the opening eight meetings in Bristol in 1984 most of us were praising God for a great start to the exhausting summer of stadium meetings. On the Saturday evening the team dispersed for a couple of days before we were due to begin the series of meetings in Sunderland. I had driven home to join my family in Surrey and was expecting to drive up to Sunderland on the Wednesday. The phone rang. 'Mr Graham would like you to join him on the train journey to Sunderland,' I was told by a youthful American voice. (To the team it is always 'Mr' Graham, never 'Doctor'.)

It wasn't convenient, but Billy is one of those men that you jump for. Once on the train I discovered the reason why I had been invited. Billy was dissatisfied with his preaching at Bristol and wanted to take his sermons apart and get things right for Sunderland. When one of his associates remonstrated that he hadn't done at all badly I saw the only touch of iron in the man that emerged all summer. 'No!' he almost snapped. 'You *know* it wasn't good. I've got to do better . . .'

This professionalism is matched by his team. Cliff Barrows gives the impression of being relaxed and easygoing, but he knows precisely what he wants to achieve and he knows exactly how to achieve it. All through the meetings when Cliff is not conducting the choir or introducing items at the podium he is watching the timing, checking on sound and any possible crowd-control matters by means of a field telephone by his side. When the television crew is in operation there are more calls and checks to be made. And while the meeting is in progress anything is likely to be changed.

From the front row, no one would guess that any of this is going on.

The unsung heroes of the Graham organisation are the follow-up team. Led by a former oil-rig worker with the appropriate name of Charlie Riggs, their job is to see that everyone who comes forward in response to the evangelist's invitation is counselled and followed through to the local church. To do this thousands of counsellors have to be trained to work within set procedures and hundreds of volunteers have to be supervised in clerical procedures. Every crusade they conduct means that a new squad involving many hundreds of people has to be motivated and trained from scratch. And every time it seems to go like clockwork.

And so I could go on developing this point, but my purpose is not to extol but to learn lessons and this one desperately needs to be learnt by British Christians. The sad fact is that not only are we desperately amateurish in most of our Christian ministry, we positively rejoice in this unprofessional approach. Some of the more pious come out with phrases like 'unspiritual' and 'trying to do the Holy Spirit's work for him' when confronted with the sorts of things that I have been describing, but it will not do. If you love someone you do your best for them and I am quite convinced that far too many of us are not doing our best for God.

What Billy Graham and his team do best – and therefore where we have most to learn – is organising and conducting evangelistic meetings. In the remaining pages of this chapter I want to share some of the lessons I have learnt from working alongside them and experiencing their 'professionalism'.

On the surface, the most remarkable feature of Billy's ministry is the 'invitation'. For some forty years, whenever he has called people 'to get up out of their seats and come forward to receive Christ', hundreds and thousands have responded. In Sunderland in 1984 we saw 14.5 per cent of those attending respond on a cold May evening.

What is the secret? I believe that Billy has a particular gift from God in this area and that is something beyond analysis and imitation. I also believe there is another more mundane reason. *More uncommitted and seeking people come to his meetings than to the meetings of any other evangelist I know.*

There are two reasons for this. The first is that Billy Graham has become a 'name' and that his reputation draws not only those who are curious but also a considerable number of those who are actually 'wanting to respond to Christ'. They are looking for a format to come to belief. 'I know,' he once told me, 'that there are people who come to our meetings who have already made up their minds to come forward.'

Towards the end of his life this same phenomenon was beginning to be seen in the ministry of David Watson. It is an almost unfair fact of life that as an evangelist becomes better known and trusted, he or she gets better 'results'. Those of us who are either new to the task or relatively unknown usually find ourselves preaching to smaller percentages of unconverted people.

But there is another factor in all this. The Billy Graham

team have learned how to organise so that there is the greatest likelihood of a large percentage of unconverted people attending their meetings. They start with prayer because, at the heart of their planning, they are genuinely spiritual.

They then seek to unite and motivate rank-and-file church people because the key to the exercise is praying people who bring others to the meetings. At the heart of their strategy is 'Operation Andrew'. They claim that they learned the idea from the English in the 1950s. The idea is based on the episode of Christ's ministry recorded in the first chapter of St John's Gospel. When Andrew met Jesus his first reaction was to seek out his brother Peter and bring him to meet Christ also. Thus as the Graham team mobilise individual Christians they implant this vision of doing what Andrew did and seeking out others to bring to the meetings. Every crusade supporter gets a prayer-card with spaces to write in the names of people to pray for and to invite and to bring.

This emphasis on the small is balanced by an unashamed readiness to plan and spend on a big-scale promotion. They unashamedly push Billy Graham's name. The posters (as we shall see in a later chapter) centre on the name. Over the years they have played down mention of '1,000-voice choirs' and the names of other participants. It is Billy Graham who is the spokesman and it is for him that they want people to come.

I believe this is right theologically and that it is a false piety that talks about 'glorifying a man'. It is also right psychologically. The vast majority of people outside our churches have chosen so to be. They are not interested in coming to a united-church project as such. They are more likely to come and hear a *person* who they suspect might have something valuable to say. They will certainly be intrigued that a group of people have so much confidence in that person's ability that they have put him in a large building and plastered his face all over the place.

People are interested in people more than philosophies and principles. The Graham team know this and have no qualms about basing their advertising on the fact. Their intention is to make it as easy as possible for the rank-and-file Christian to say to his or her unbelieving friend, 'Why not come with me and hear Billy Graham?' If it helps – and especially where the evangelist is less well known – they will finance popular magazine-type publications that tell the story of his life and ministry.

'I would rather not see my name all over the place,' I have heard Billy say on several occasions. 'When we get to heaven the "big names" there will be people you and I have never heard of. But I know that we need to have this sort of publicity to get the people to come and hear the Gospel.'

What happens when people actually arrive at the meeting-place is carefully thought through. Cliff Barrows and Billy Graham have tried to design a meeting which will put the uncommitted person at ease. Relatively little is sung by the congregation and the songs and hymns chosen need to score points on two counts. First, if at all possible, they should be well-known by those who don't come to church regularly. That rules out most of the new songs and choruses unless they are very easily learnt.

Second, they must not contain words that embarrass the outsider and make him feel he does not belong. Cliff will try to avoid congregational items which call upon everyone to sing such personalised statements as 'I worship ... I adore ... I praise your name ...'

What Cliff looks for are the most objective types of wording to put into the mouths of those who might be conscious of their state of unbelief. The more subjective or worshipful songs he will ask the choir to sing, so that the spirit of joyous belief can still be experienced by all present.

Learning from Billy

In a sense, Cliff does not try to force everyone present to be a *participant*. If they want to remain *spectators* and feel more comfortable in such a role, that is allowable.

This is a lesson which needs to be learnt by many British evangelists and those who plan their meetings. The churches, and especially the Christian youth scenes, have a host of new worship songs. Most are tuneful, and fun to sing. Many are deeply worshipful – even moving. 'This,' many say, 'is where the Spirit is at work. The world needs to see us celebrating our faith. The outsiders need to experience their sense of being outside our peace and joy. It will convict them. It will make them seek God!'

A whole theory of 'celebration evangelism' has been built on this. There are some who believe that there is a particular power that is released from God when his people praise him.

It sounds good, but I do not believe it is true. I believe half the problem is that we Christians enjoy doing these things ourselves and that we tend to rationalise and theologise from what we enjoy doing. A frequent complaint about the Mission England meetings in 1984 and 1985 was that they were 'nothing special' – even 'flat'. I believe these criticisms reveal a lack of understanding of the minds and attitudes of those who do not yet believe.

The most important part of the planning of the evening is that people are not kept waiting to hear Billy speak. Within thirty-five minutes of the start he will be on his feet. It is to hear him that people have come. They have *not* come to worship God. Many of them cannot yet do that. What they *can* do is listen to the Gospel.

Thus soloists, testimonies and notices are kept to a minimum. Billy Graham is acutely aware that it is the evening and that many in front of him have had a hard day. He wants people to be as alert as possible to face up to the challenge of the Gospel.

Here again present trends in British evangelism must

come under scrutiny. We are – I dare to believe – more creative and imaginative than the American evangelicals. We have some remarkable musicians. We have explored approaches to drama, dance, mime and poetry. Above all we love bands on the platform leading up-tempo Christian songs. Give us a chance and we fill up an hour before the evangelist stands up to speak.

I have myself on a couple of occasions been expected to begin a sermon over ninety minutes after the start of a meeting. At some meetings the sermon has almost seemed an afterthought, and even been upstaged by some of the other things on the programme.

To be blunt, it smacks more of Christian self-indulgence than sensitive evangelism.

Billy Graham's meetings are first and foremost *functional*. They are designed to be the end of the process which begins when individual Christians start praying and then invite their friends to hear the Gospel. It does not surprise me in the slightest if Christians say that there are more exciting and enjoyable ways to worship God. There are.

But what has that got to do with what is meant to be an introduction exercise to the Christian faith?

The visits of Dr Graham and his team in 1984 and 1985 brought considerable blessing to thousands of lives. If evangelists and those who plan evangelistic meetings in this country could be humble enough to learn some lessons from the way they worked there could be blessings in the future that might even outweigh those we received from those historic visits.

6

Why isn't there a British Billy Graham?

It was one of the first radio interviews I did after the news had broken about Mission England. The opening question came like a bullet and practically routed me. 'Why,' I was asked aggressively, 'bring in an American evangelist? Haven't we got good enough evangelists of our own?'

It was an eminently sensible question to ask. Why, indeed, when we wanted a figurehead evangelistic preacher for Mission England did we have to look overseas?

Two things must be made clear immediately. First, Britain is not short of gifted evangelists. Every year there is a national conference for evangelists run by the Evangelical Alliance and some 200 people turn up. Many of them, it is true, work in very small dimensions. They would not pretend to have the same sort of ministry as the famous American preacher.

There are, however, a growing number of evangelists in the United Kingdom who do have the gifts, I believe, to preach to large crowds and to make the good news of Jesus Christ relevant and challenging. I can think of half-a-dozen men, any one of whom is capable of the sort of ministry Billy Graham has exercised. Why is it not happening?

The second thing that needs to be made clear is this: evangelism is not primarily about 'big-name' evangelists.

All Christians are called to be witnesses to the reality and meaning of Jesus Christ and the natural, everyday sharing of this good news is the true evangelism. The majority of people become Christians, not through specific activities we can label as 'evangelistic', but through relationships with ordinary Christians. As I shall state in a later chapter the three most-mentioned reasons for why people have become Christians are all about relationships over a period of time.

The most-mentioned reason is a relationship to a nearby church. The second most-mentioned reason is through relationships with a Christian or Christians within the family. The third most-mentioned reason is through the influence of a Christian friend.

Having said this, it is also clear from the New Testament that God gives a particular gift of evangelism to individual people. The Epistle to the Ephesians mentions 'evangelists' as one of the specifically gifted ministries in the Church. When an evangelist is properly used he or she does more than a solo effort in commending the faith. An evangelist, by doing his or her own evangelism, creates the conditions in which the witnessing of others is easier to do.

This is certainly the case with Billy Graham. The fact that he is in town preaching the Gospel, heightens public awareness of the Gospel in the community at large. He dramatises his own agenda and as a result local Christians can take advantage of greater awareness of and openness to the Gospel. This in turn leads more Christians, naturally, to invite many of the unconvinced to come and hear.

In today's highly developed society, communication is strictly channelled through press, radio, TV and public meetings. The individual with something to say all too easily gets lost and feels like someone shouting into a dream. If breakthroughs into public awareness are to be made it will have to be through gifted, individual people. It makes sense to me to expect God to raise up one or two key evangelists

Why isn't there a British Billy Graham?

able to capture the imagination of many and to be focal-point people whose very presence dramatises their message.

So why has Britain not got its own big-name evangelists? I believe there are two reasons.

The first is to do with attitudes in the churches. Christians of any nationality carry into their Christianity characteristics of their particular cultures. Sometimes these characteristics can be 'baptised' and are enhancing. Sometimes they are unhelpful and need to be discarded.

The British people in the late twentieth century seem to be infected by ever-increasing degrees of scepticism and readiness to criticise and debunk. We very quickly feel that some much vaunted scheme or product is 'too good to be true', and that some much praised and prominent person is 'too big for his boots'.

There are many good features in this national characteristic. We are unlikely to encourage dictators! The unfortunate side-effects are that enthusiasts (whether it be in industry or in the Church) get too little encouragement. This affects the development of Christian speakers with the sort of flair and forthrightness that a large-meeting evangelist needs.

The Americans on the other hand are great affirmers and enthusiasts. They admire innovators and applaud a good salesman. I remember negotiating for the English rights of a book with an American publisher. It was not a great scoop and no great sums of money were involved. Nevertheless, when I had finally stated my price and the deal was struck, he jumped up with genuine pleasure and grabbed my hand. 'It's nice doing business with you' is the catch-phrase – and very often the words are said with genuine conviction.

Of course, this enthusiastic, open and relatively uncritical spirit has its unhelpful spin-offs. Most of the weird religious cults seem to start in America! The positive outworking, however, is that when a man like Billy Graham emerges there are people who get behind him to support and promote.

I have no doubts that Billy has a very particular gift from God. Perhaps – in this age of a shrinking world – there is only room for one such person at a time. However, I am convinced that several highly-gifted British evangelists could have become – as Dr Graham is in America – public figures if they had been given the encouragement and financial support that they deserved.

But material help and expertise are not enough in themselves. The statesman-evangelist needs to enjoy a broad measure of respect across the churches. The reasons why Billy Graham was invited to be chief spokesman for Mission England were threefold. The first was that, as an international figure, he was likely to attract far more media attention than any British evangelist. The second reason was that he was likely to command more respect across all the Christian traditions than any evangelist that the British could put into the field. The third reason was that he was far and away the most experienced evangelist in history in leading the sort of project we had in mind.

Wisdom after the event suggests another factor which played a greater part than we anticipated. Dr Graham is surrounded by the most experienced team of mission-preparation and logistics people that can be found anywhere. I came to see how essential it is for a large-scale evangelist to have this sort of back-up team.

A city-wide mission requires the mobilisation of the resources of a high percentage of that city's churches. If this is to happen then there has to be a high degree of trust and respect for the missioner. Very few British evangelists have been given that amount of trust.

In recent years it was beginning to be seen with the remarkable David Watson. An awesomely committed and extremely gracious man, he was able to draw support across a wide spectrum. However, his gentle but unhidden advocacy of charismatic renewal did not please some who would normally support evangelistic enterprises, and his openness to participation alongside Roman Catholics disturbed others.

We shall never know whether David would have graduated to leading ever-larger missions and projects. He died when one felt there was more land to be possessed, and many of us still find difficulty in understanding why the Lord took such a gifted and lovely man so early in his life.

Apart from David Watson, no British evangelist since Tom Rees in the 1940s and 1950s has inspired such confidence – although several deserve to. Because evangelical Christianity is a minority group within the overall British religious scene, it is not easy for an evangelist (nearly all of whom come from this tradition) to attract a wide enough base for large-scale missions.

However, the problem is compounded by the fact that the evangelical minority in Britain is, in reality, a fragmented community. It is difficult for an evangelist to unite his or her own natural constituency. For example, there are some evangelicals who will not tolerate co-operation with other Christian groupings who do not hold a particular view of the inspiration and authority of Scripture. There are other evangelical Christians who would insist that evangelistic preaching without an overt place for healing and a particular view of the infilling of God's Holy Spirit is unbiblical and deficient. Such people are growing in number. Still more evangelicals, however, take fright at such a position and would find it hard to support a venture with this charismatic emphasis.

There are also many evangelicals who are sceptical of the place of 'crusade evangelism' and are likely only to give half-hearted support. It is therefore not easy for an evangelist to emerge who has the confidence of the bulk of the evangelical community, let alone can draw support from other traditions.

My observation is that most of our evangelists either share the non-co-operative scruples I have mentioned above or are emerging from the charismatic stable. This means that they are not likely to draw large numbers of uncommitted people to their meetings.

As I pointed out in an earlier chapter, the evangelical and charismatic communities tend to be the most entrenched and inward-looking expressions of Christianity in the United Kingdom. They are hyperactive and this excessive activity tends to tie up the socialising time of their members. This in turn leads to a lack of contact and sympathy with non-Christians. The total effect of this mix is that an evangelist relying solely on support from such churches is hardly likely to preach to high percentages of unconverted people.

But surely, it might be argued, an evangelist is someone who preaches to those who do not belong to existing congregations? Surely it does not matter whether he is supported by many or by few churches?

The answer to these reactions is clear. The evangelist does and *should* depend on church support. He or she is someone whose ministry is a gift from God *to* the Church. Evangelists who try to act independently of close co-operation with local churches are likely to do more harm than good. The churches need the ministry of evangelists, but evangelists also need the continuous pastoral and outreaching work of congregations.

It is the churches that reach out to the uncommitted and unconverted and bring them to hear the evangelist. The effectiveness of any evangelist is in direct relationship to the effectiveness of the churches in doing this. If a mission is supported by a small number of churches, each of which is so organised that its members have little time to make and keep natural friendships, that mission will be a flop. It does not matter how able and gifted the evangelist is – it will flop.

Why isn't there a British Billy Graham?

The greater the number of churches involved the greater the chance that a large number of unconverted people will hear the evangelist. But these chances are reduced if the churches involved have an entrenched mentality.

It is impossible to discuss the question of large-scale evangelism without facing up to the thorny problems of co-operation between churches of differing viewpoints. Those evangelists who feel it is wrong to co-operate with Christians who differ (say on the Bible) will inevitably limit the dimensions of their ministry. Sometimes the problem such evangelists face is not one that they feel personally but one imposed on them by their supporters or the people who take initiatives in extending invitations.

I have set out my own views on co-operation in an earlier chapter. For me the key factor is that the evangelist is allowed to be true to himself or herself. It is simply out of the question to ask an evangelist to preach within doctrinal guidelines laid down by an organising committee so that as many Christian groupings as possible can feel accommodated.

At the same time I feel it is equally wrong to move in the opposite direction so that the organisers of a mission only allow the co-operation of those who will sign some doctrinal basis. I don't see any grounds for this in the New Testament. There the basis for hearing the Gospel is simply the desire to hear it. When Jesus sent out the seventy-two he told them to go and teach where that teaching was welcomed (Matt. 10). In the Acts of the Apostles we see Peter wrestling with the problem of who should be allowed to co-operate with the proclamation of the Gospel (Acts 10). Cornelius, a man of deficient doctrinal understanding, invited Peter to preach. God significantly gave Peter a vision to clarify the rightness of accepting such an invitation. The meeting took place. A great impact was made, and presumably it was Cornelius who was left to follow what had been begun.

I believe we are always trying to 'protect' God against the messy ways in which his Holy Spirit seems to work! The fact of the matter is that the preaching of the Gospel *changes* situations. It can change those who are brought along because someone judges they want to hear, and it can also change those who brought such people along!

For me the key factor in co-operative evangelism is whether a church is prepared to support the evangelist in 'doing his thing' and preaching the message to which he is committed. I should want to extend the evangelist's 'thing' to include the immediate follow-up and nurture of those who respond. If a church is happy to do that then I should welcome such co-operation.

It is not a perfect solution to genuine problems, but there is no perfect solution this side of heaven. And in heaven there is no need for evangelism!

There is a second and totally different factor that has inhibited the rise of British evangelists capable of leading large events. This is the average seating capacity of the average town- or city-centre auditorium.

We have very few covered venues in Britain with a seating capacity above 2,000 or so. Most town halls, sports centres and cinemas seem to stop at around 1,500 seats.

This means that our biggest meetings are still fairly small – but the side-effects of these limitations are more subtle and far-reaching. When an evangelist comes to lead a mission in a 1,000- or 2,000-seater hall the problem is not how to get 'bottoms on to seats'. The problem is how to keep the wrong bottoms off the seats! The local Christian community can usually fill such a venue night after night without much serious attempt to draw in the unbeliever or seeker.

In other words, British evangelists are far too often preaching to the converted!

This leads to some undesirable consequences. First the evangelist finds himself compelled to carry *two* agendas. He

Why isn't there a British Billy Graham? 89

has his natural agenda to want to speak to the unconverted, but he feels he cannot overlook the fact that most of his hearers have other needs. Inevitably, therefore, he finds himself engaging in a teaching or renewal ministry. Equally inevitably, the desires and preferences of the majority in front of him tend to dictate the terms with regard to the nature of the meeting.

Very easily we end up with evangelists presiding over jamborees for Christians.

I remember being rebuked at the end of an evangelistic meeting in the De Montford Hall, Leicester. I had closed the meeting immediately after my talk with a prayer of commitment and asked those who had prayed the prayer to come forward and meet me and receive some simple counselling.

A small queue formed. The third or fourth person in the queue, however, had not come to be counselled. She had come to tell me that I had let the Holy Spirit down in not closing the meeting with a great hymn of praise and worship. There were about ten or so potential converts behind her, but that was irrelevant to her purpose. She, as a Christian, had not got what she wanted and the evangelist needed to be rebuked. It was a heartbreaking and hurtful experience which I have never forgotten.

At the heart of the ministry of most evangelists is the invitation to a response. Billy Graham is famous for his call that people should 'get up out of their seats' and come forward to 'receive Christ'. But Billy is essentially a single-agenda evangelist conscious of the presence of many who recognise that they are still unconverted. What happens to the invitation of the double-agenda evangelist in a jamboree for Christians?

Almost inevitably it becomes a call to a multiple response – conversion – rededication – filling with the Spirit – commitment to service – inner healing and even more. It is hard not to conclude that the essential currency is being debased and that one is encouraging a sort of Christian growth-by-crisis theology.

In an odd way, therefore, one of the best things that could happen for the cause of British evangelists is the building of a chain of auditoriums around the country with seating for between 5,000 and 10,000 people!

In the meantime, perhaps we need to be more adventurous in the use of portable structures and in converting places like warehouses and hangars.

Am I saying in all this that if we changed a few attitudes and built bigger halls we could 'make' a British Billy Graham? No. What I am saying is that Britain is not an ideal place to develop the potential of a statesman-evangelist if such a person exists.

The prior question, of course, is this. Has God given the British churches a person with such a potential ministry? Is he doing so now? I believe the answer to both questions is – yes.

To be frank, I believe the British churches failed to recognise what God had given them in Tom Rees and David Watson. I fear that should God raise any successors (and I can think of a few candidates) the churches would probably fail again.

7

Parables and Posters

In the summer of 1984 thousands of posters went up all over England. The colour scheme was red, black and white – national colours. The design was dominated by a photograph of Billy Graham and it simply read: *Billy Graham – worth listening to*. At the bottom of the poster were details of the nearest meetings at which he was to speak.

In 1985 the same posters appeared again, mainly in the South Yorkshire area, advertising the Mission England meetings in Sheffield, but also in relation to the fifty-one localised relay centres linked to Sheffield by the European communications satellite.

These posters – which appeared on hoardings, in newspapers, outside churches and on the sides of buses – seemed astonishingly simple and perhaps even bland, yet they were the product of a great deal of what some call 'doing theology'. There are important lessons to learn from that exercise and I wish to share them here.

It is not every day that an Anglican clergyman is put in charge of a national advertising campaign with a budget of many thousands of pounds. Rather than brief an advertising agency I felt we needed to bring together an *ad hoc* media and publicity committee of convinced Christians who were all involved professionally in modern communications. John Capon, the religious correspondent of the *Sunday Telegraph* and in charge of advertising and public relations with Tear Fund, was chairman. Christopher Rees, a BBC radio producer, Derek Williams, then editor of *Today* magazine, John Attwater an advertising account executive and Frank Lawton, head of a creative design agency, made up the membership. Ronald Allison of Thames TV and formerly press officer to the Queen received the papers of the committee and offered advice to us. Bob Williams of the Billy Graham organisation and I sat in on all sessions.

We tried to think out what advertising could and should do in relation to the planned Billy Graham meetings. We tried to put ourselves into the shoes of those who might pass a poster in the street. As Christians we wanted to ask whether there was a specifically 'Christian' way of advertising.

At this point one factor needs to be faced. We are living in a very different sort of society from that of Jesus and the first Christians. To say piously that Jesus, Peter, Paul and the rest never advertised and yet people came to hear them, is to say something both true and rather silly. It is true that they did not design and put up posters. Nobody did in those days. It is *not* true that their activities were not advertised. They *were* advertised, and by the best means possible – through the gossip of a talking community!

Up to the Industrial Revolution most communities were small and the ways of life necessitated continuous conversation. People did not move around encapsulated in the private worlds of motor cars. People didn't mail order for their supplies. People hadn't privatised means of entertainment and information such as radio and television.

News travelled and good news travelled fast. And a little assistance to the process didn't come amiss. When George Whitfield preached in the open at Moorfields outside London, a rash of hastily printed posters were put up around the city to advertise the fact.

Today's world is very different. In spite of the fact that we

Parables and Posters

are living through a 'communications revolution' it is very difficult to get news to move an inch unless some contrived means of communication is harnessed. News doesn't travel, it has to be *sent*.

What we wanted to do in the advertising campaign for the Mission England Billy Graham meetings was to 'turbo-charge gossip'! We wanted to create the same effect in a modern community as would have happened naturally in first-century Judea when John the Baptist was in the vicinity.

Our first attempt was to use a photograph of Billy Graham's face alongside a challenging quote of something he had said. Underneath would come the almost throwaway but (we hoped) provoking words: 'worth listening to'. We hoped this phrase might catch on and lead to conversations all over the country not only about the evangelist but about the Gospel also. It put the focus on both man and message.

A first set of 'roughs' was produced to display to representatives from the six centres where Billy would preach. The biggest problem was that we found it difficult to get genuine quotations from things that Billy Graham had said or had written which would have impact within the confines of a poster. We had hoped to convey a tantalising snatch of the sort of things that Billy says, but we ended up with phrases that hardly 'grabbed'. A sermon, article or book calls for one way of talking – advertising copy is something else!

When the first set of roughs were shown to the regional representatives there was a problem. They were so well executed (in spite of being roughs) that people were impressed – too easily impressed. Most of those present felt a little awed by the professionalism of Frank Lawton's design agency work that they virtually passed it on the nod. Better copy was needed for the quotes, they said, a little more sense of 'invitation' to the meeting perhaps; but that was all. Copies of the various designs were taken back to local committees who, in turn, were invited to send in further feed-back.

All seemed to be going through on the nod when the co-ordinator of one of our regional offices phoned. His region was not happy, he said. They had commissioned their own designer. Their alternative designs were to be brought to the next meeting of our *ad hoc* media and publicity committee.

I think I ought to state two things at this point. The first is that at the time I was upset by this move and I shall state in the paragraphs to come where I felt the alternative ideas were wrong. The second point is that, on reflection, I am very grateful for the region's reaction because it opened up the right issues and it led to a better set of final designs.

When the alternative concept for our advertising campaign was presented we saw that it was based on a number of basic attitudes. First, the advertisements should not glorify a man; second, Mission England was a three-year project of the churches and the name was over a year old and becoming known. The designs from the *ad hoc* committee did not mention Mission England or display its logo. Prominent use of the name would encourage Christians. Third, with so much money about to be invested in the campaign it was wrong not to use the exposure to preach the Gospel in some more direct manner. Fourth, the black, red and white designs were too dull. More colours were needed in these days of full-colour advertising.

The alternative designs – in rough form – were well designed. The words 'Mission England' were set in larger type than the words 'Billy Graham'. On some versions of the design a facsimile page from the Bible emerged with a key verse on the content of the Gospel visible and legible for all to read. Running through all designs was the slogan 'God knows there's a better way!'

A vigorous discussion took place between the committee and representatives from the region. At one point, with reference to my objections to using verses of Scripture, I was accused of 'being ashamed of the Gospel'. The man who said

Parables and Posters

those words is now a good friend of mine and was not trying to be unkind. He was simply stating things as he saw them. On reflection I think it was a pity that more people from all the regions were not in attendance, because that committee meeting was forced to 'do theology'. It was also forced to face up to some uncomfortable realities behind some of our apparently pious attitudes. It was forced to ask – how do you *broadcast* the Gospel, and, indeed, can it be broadcast?

As a result of the meeting I circulated a report to the publicity committees of all the other regions together with a multiple choice 'test' paper to try to get people to face up to the realities of advertising. Here are some of the questions I asked.

1. Who do you think the advertising campaign should be aimed at?
    (a) The general public
    (b) Church people
    (c) Both
2. What do you want the campaign to achieve?
    (a) To publicise Mission England
    (b) To preach the Gospel
    (c) To alert people that they can hear Billy Graham near by
3. The alternative proposals major on a strong catch-phrase, 'God knows there's a better way'. Do you
    (a) like it?
    (b) dislike it?
    (c) worry about apparent blasphemy?
4. Write 1, 2, 3, 4 etc. beside the objectives of the campaign listed below to indicate your group's priorities.
    (a) Preach the gospel
    (b) Get people to the meetings
    (c) Encourage Christians
    (d) Publicise Mission England
    (e) Get people talking about the Gospel

5. Write down the order of interest that the general public is likely to show in the following.
   (a) Christianity
   (b) Mission England
   (c) Billy Graham
   (d) The Churches

What I was trying to do in this exercise was to force Christians to try to look at our advertising campaign *from the starting-point of the casual glance of the average non-church-goer who was walking along a busy street*. What was something called 'Mission England' to him or her? What time was there to stop and read a text of Scripture (or any other prolonged piece of writing, including our original idea of a quotation from Billy)? And, if the words were read, what assumptions would such a person bring into the reading?

Ninety per cent of the people of England do not think a weekly visit to church is worth the effort. 'Church' is either a turn-off or a yawn for most of them. Many feel they are excluded from church for social reasons. On the other hand, people are interested in people. Anyone who looked human enough, and whose face people felt worth slapping on hoardings all over town, would at least give rise to curiosity. It was important to lodge the name in people's minds plus the thought that he was worth listening to. *That* is what gossip does. It doesn't preach, it names names and passes on opinions.

There were two other factors we knew we could be sure of. The first was that in the area where Billy Graham was going to preach and where the posters were going up, there were thousands of Christians who knew more than the posters were telling and were bursting to have a chance to tell! Further, as Christians, they were (we hoped) even more motivated to talk about Billy Graham's message – the Gospel. We wanted people to get into conversations with living agents of Christ, not with inanimate advertisements.

The second factor was that we knew that by the time those

Parables and Posters

posters were in public view there would have been local newspaper articles, and items on radio and television. We also were planning a massive distribution of leaflets to millions of homes in the regions involved. These would be more explicit. Thus the cumulative effect of all these elements had to be taken into account when one judged whether we were being ashamed of the Gospel.

In passing, it is worth recording that the designer who put together the rival set of designs and challenged the central committee was entrusted with the design of the visitation handbill, and a very good job he made of it. Again, our final designs were brighter and stronger and less cluttered as a result of the debate. Yes – and we did find a place to insert the Mission England logo.

When the time came and Billy Graham arrived to speak in Bristol, over 90 per cent of those interviewed by Gallup poll were aware that he was in town and over *60 per cent* felt he had something relevant to say to the people of Britain.

But where's the theology in all this talk of working out posters from the point of view of the casual glance of the man in the street? The whole exercise took me back to the writing of my book, *The Gagging of God*. As part of my thinking at the time I was driven back to ask why Jesus spoke in parables when he faced the crowds – the equivalent of our passing man or woman in the street glancing at posters.

There is a great deal of misunderstanding about parables, especially among evangelical Christians. Most people seem to think that they were homely illustrations to make Jesus's teaching relevant and more easily understood. The truth of the matter is exactly the reverse. The parables were deliberate acts of oblique rather than direct communication.

One evidence of this is that they often puzzled the Lord's own close followers. After Jesus had told his parable about the wheat and the weeds (tares) we read that, 'His disciples came to him and said, "Explain to us the parable of the weeds in the field" ' (Matt. 13:36). Clearly the sense was lost on them also, which hardly commends the effectiveness of the parable as an illustration to make things clearer.

On another occasion, recorded in John 16:29, the disciples acknowledged that 'Now you are speaking clearly and without figures of speech.' So why did Jesus not speak clearly at all times? Is it not even more surprising that it was precisely when Jesus had his biggest audiences that he chose to speak most obliquely? Matthew's Gospel records (13:34): 'Jesus spoke all these things to the crowd in parables; he did not say anything to them without using a parable.'

The truth was that the crowds, unlike the disciples who had 'left all to follow' Jesus were not ready to receive what Jesus really wanted to say to them. If he had spoken plainly their unseeking minds would have rejected what was said. Every rejection makes the next rejection easier. Before long rejection of the truth can become a habit. When people are not ready to think about the Christian message with an open heart and mind, then precious truths will be spurned. As Jesus put it, it will be like casting pearls before pigs (Matt. 7:6).

The vast majority of those crowds who came to hear Jesus were curious and little more. They were not ready to follow. When Jesus used parables he was partly being judgmental. Speaking to his followers he said:

> The knowledge of the secrets of the kingdom of heaven has been given to you, but not to them . . .
> This is why I speak to them in parables.
> 'Though seeing, they do not see;
> though hearing, they do not hear or understand.'
> In them is fulfilled the prophecy of Isaiah:
> 'You will be ever hearing but never understanding . . .
> For this people's heart has become calloused; they hardly hear with their ears, and they have closed their eyes' (Matt. 13:11–15).

Parables and Posters

Thus we find the constant use of a phrase alongside the parables. Jesus would say: 'He who has ears, let him hear.' The person in the crowd with 'ears' would see in the parable something that would stimulate him to seek further. So the parable was also a merciful tactic. It ensured that there was not careless rejection of precious truths and yet gave help to those who were looking for answers.

It was my argument, therefore, at the media and publicity committee, and especially in the creative dispute over the alternative concept, that we must not put pearls before pigs. To try to preach the Gospel from the publicity was to run the risk of reinforcing rejection – the very opposite of our purpose in the Billy Graham meetings. What we needed to do was to stimulate an appetite that might lead to people coming to hear.

The phrase 'God knows there's a better way' was nearly right, but I opposed it because there was the danger of offence to Christians who might regard the 'God knows' *double entendre* as blasphemous. There was, however, another problem – it mentioned the name of God. It may come as a surprise to many, but Jesus, in his parables, did not talk about God. He talked about 'lords', 'kings', 'fathers' and 'farmers' and he who had ears would hear and make the connection.

I believe we are touching here on something very important for the whole task of communicating the Gospel. We need to ask not 'are we talking about God too little', but *'are we talking about God too much?'* Familiarity breeds contempt and religious matters are no exception. Only about 10 per cent of British people call themselves atheists. The problem is that the vast majority of people outside the churches are prepared to give God the benefit of their doubts. The problem is either that they already think they know what the God package means (and have dismissed it as of no immediate concern) or that they know they are deliberately rejecting it. To shout texts at them from the hoardings and bus sides will hardly help and might even harden.

What we have to do when we are 'speaking' to the uncommitted is to stimulate a searching spirit. Our purpose in the advertising campaign was to create awareness, arouse curiosity and to make it easier for invitations to the meetings to be made and to be accepted.

We also wanted it to stimulate discussion and to create opportunities and openings for Christians to share their own personal faith. We wanted the end-product of all this to be that Billy Graham was only one of a number of voices commending Christ from the heart. We were convinced that Christianity is 'caught' from enthusiastic believers more than 'taught'. Jesus made his converts not so much from preaching at them but from inviting them to accompany him. Words, of course, are essential throughout the entire process, and even more so now when no physical Jesus is with us; but *people* are the best sermons.

When we break away from planning evangelistic campaigns how do we apply these insights? In *The Gagging of God* I urged that Christians needed to be in the media and to be in the ranks of dramatists, novelists and songwriters. These are the people who preach today's parables. I remember singer/songwriter Garth Hewitt saying, 'my job is to sow doubts in the minds of agnostics'. I would add that we need more Christians in the teaching profession and in the social services; not to be fervently seeking opportunities to 'preach' but to be living parables where they are and as they influence people.

However, the moment one starts naming groups in society in this manner the more one sees this as a calling to all. We are called to live the sorts of lives that lead others to seek the Christ we profess to follow. We are called to be and to do what will give others the appetite to hear the Gospel. And one thing that does *not* create an appetite is the continuous offering of food. That can make people feel sick.

This, I know, is dangerous talk. The problem we face

Parables and Posters

overall is that too many Christians are too reluctant to speak of their faith. That must be remedied. However, many evangelicals are, I believe, too eager to press their faith on others when the time is inappropriate. That can be just as ineffective and carries with it the additional disadvantage of injuring other people's chances of being in the right condition to seek Christ and to give the Gospel the hearing it deserves.

One useful lesson I learned from Malcolm Saunders, British head of *Evangelism Explosion*, is this: Always ask permission before developing any point about Christ. In the account of Philip and the Ethiopian (Acts 8) it is the non-believer who dictates the agenda of the discussion that was to lead to his ultimate conversion. Philip, for his part, created the opportunity by the use of a question when he saw the eunuch reading Scripture: 'Do you understand what you are reading?' (v. 30). He then waited for the invitation to sit alongside and discuss the passage.

When someone is enthusiastic to put across a message, asking permission and waiting for invitations doesn't come easily.

To revert to the Mission England meetings, however, when people responded to the advertising and to the personal invitations and went to hear Billy Graham, that meant they had given the preacher permission to preach. They were saying that they had 'ears to hear' and when people say that, the time for parables has passed and the time for direct speaking and earnest advocacy has come.

8

Churches that Evangelise

It is always illuminating to ask Christians how they arrived at such a position of commitment and understanding.

The great danger for those of us who are enthusiastic about 'doing' evangelism is that we start at the wrong end. We tend to believe that something we want to do will get the desired effect, namely people coming to a point of commitment. What we need to consider is the other side of the story. What approaches, techniques, preachers or whatever have a track record of effectiveness?

A few years ago I decided to conduct a simple survey. Wherever I was to address a meeting of Christians I would try to discover the factors behind their own conversions. I soon learnt that for most people there was no *single* factor that accounted for their conversions. After some initial chopping and changing, I hit upon the approach of listing a number of factors and asking people to give the chief reason, on reflection, as to why they had come to embrace the Christian faith. If they found it hard to give a single reason, they were allowed two votes and no more.

I soon found as I used this approach that the results worked out practically the same wherever I went. I would put up an overhead projector slide with my accumulated totals for each of the listed factors masked out. We would then conduct the survey in the meeting by asking for a show

Churches that Evangelise

of hands to each suggested factor set out on the slide. I would enter the findings of the meeting against each heading and with a final flourish remove the mask that covered the accumulated totals so that those present could compare their findings against the developing picture from around the country. The results nearly always matched exactly!

What, then, were the findings of this survey? When I called a halt to the exercise and worked out the findings as percentages (with thanks to a teenage son who was better at statistics than I am) this is how it appeared.

		per cent
1.	The influence of a particular church over a period of time	27.8
2.	The influence of other members of one's own family	25.8
3.	The influence of a Christian friend or friends	19.9
4.	A specific evangelistic event or activity	13.2

Nothing else came anywhere near and I have to say that I think the percentage for specific evangelism is slightly flattering in the light of the fact that the largest meeting at which I conducted the survey contained an astoundingly high percentage of people who put this as one of their two chief reasons.

The thing that, for me, stands out most clearly from these results is that the vast majority of Christians come to such a position *not through some crisis, but through a process*. To put it another way, people are converted more through relationships than through techniques or special efforts.

I believe that it is most important to start our planning for evangelism from this end. One thing that the survey revealed was that very few people have been converted through *reading Christian literature*. As someone involved in publishing I find this sobering. The vast majority of books written to be 'evangelistic' and for the eyes of non-believers either never get into the hands of such people or have little effect when they do.

Christian literature is of considerable value in educating and informing Christians. Books and magazines can also inspire and be means of sharing testimony. That is their main value and we should spend our publishing budgets with that in mind.

Another more important lesson to learn from these figures is that the typical conversion is not sudden. I believe many involved in evangelism have a romantic view that the model conversion is somewhat like that of St Paul on the Damascus road. One moment everything is in darkness. The next and all is light.

I'm not sure that even Paul's conversion was that sudden. He might well have been caught up in a mental struggle for some time before the journey to Damascus. The witness of Stephen as he was being stoned to death might have started inner doubts about the rightness of his position. The very vehemence of his opposition – as sometimes happens – could be evidence not of inner conviction but uneasiness. In his testimony before Agrippa (Acts 26) Paul recalled that at the moment of encounter with Christ on the Damascus road he 'heard' the Lord saying, 'It is hard for you to kick against the goads' (v. 14). Those words would seem to indicate some inner struggle.

It is also true that Paul needed the ministrations of Ananias and the Christian Church at Damascus before he was confident enough to make a stand for the Christ he had once opposed.

We cannot, of course, be sure concerning Paul, but he is not the only Apostle in the New Testament and there is little doubt that for most of the others conversion was a case of the truth dawning upon them over a period of time. And as truth dawns on people there is usually the creation of greater openness to more of that same truth.

When we plan evangelism in the light of the process model rather than the crisis model then we are set free from having to find sure-fire 'kill-me-quick' methods of doing things. That does not mean we reject the place of evangelistic campaigns or personal witnessing aids and 'systems'. They can be very important – *within the process*.

If we are to have a strategy for more conversions, we need to ask not how can we create more *crises*, but how can we initiate and foster more *processes*. The answer is obvious. We have to start with the local church.

What we need as the foundation of a strategy for national evangelism is churches which evangelise, and which plan their evangelism with the realities and not the myths of conversion models in mind. If evangelism is not happening at local-church level then nothing significant is going to happen from evangelism attempted in any other dimension.

However, it is one thing to see and to say this. It is quite another matter to make it happen. Part of the problem is that a very large number of congregations are full of people who attend church for personal comfort and reassurance and not as part of an outgoing life of service for Christ. This personal inward-lookingness usually leads to congregational inward-lookingness.

Very many churches have become clubs for those interested in the religious side of life or who find the Christianity route to be the best for finding and maintaining a network of friendships. It has been suggested that one reason for the impressive church attendance in the United States is that in a highly mobile society people look to the churches to give them 'roots' and relationships. At least one highly effective Californian church known to me accepts this analysis and bases an effective evangelistic strategy on holding welcoming classes for new attenders.

Now I do not want to say that this club mentality in our churches is something wilful, stemming from a deliberate rejection of Christ and his call to discipleship. Club-mentality churches happen easily and subtly almost without people realising what is going on. They are yet another example of how we can look to bolthole worlds that allow us to escape from a bewilderingly impersonal society which we cannot control and which we fear will steam-roller us into being nonentities.

When attempts are made to try to change a church from inward-lookingness to outgoingness one often sees fierce and irrational resistance. More than this, one can even see people resorting to theology! Some great biblical principle is dug up from somewhere either to bolster what has already been done for years or to attack some proposed change.

Evangelism is a very threatening thing for a congregation to contemplate. It means encouraging members to confront people who do not believe. It means facing the prospect that new people may join the fellowship and by so doing, change it.

I remember preparing a talk on the conversion of St Paul. As I worked my way through the relevant section of Acts 9, I became aware that it was describing *two* conversions. Paul had to be converted to Christ and to his Church. The Church, for its part, had to be converted to Paul! The Lord not only had to meet supernaturally with Paul. He had to meet supernaturally with Ananias, leader of the Christians in Damascus. In some ways, Ananias needed more persuasion than Paul!

The more I think about it, the more I can see that a congregation needs to be converted to the converted.

A friend of mine was once curate in a housing-estate parish which was very proud of its new buildings. The church council encouraged him to run a youth mission to reach some of the 'tougher' youngsters in the area. He got hold of an empty shop-front and converted it into a coffee bar. He brought in musicians and a youth evangelist. The church prayed and was excited. Volunteers rolled up. The doors were opened. The very sorts of young people they wanted to reach, began to come.

By the time the mission was over the curate had drawn in a group of youngsters who had developed a strong interest in Christ, if not more. They had, however, no clue as to the required etiquette for behaving in church and the studded footwear of some of them was likely to damage the wooden flooring of the building.

The group came along to church, late, for a service on the Sunday following the mission. Their boots made a noise on the stairs. They kept close to each other for mutual support. They giggled and chatted because they felt uncomfortable.

They never came again. Nobody actually told them to stay away, but they picked up the message. The church was not able to face a conversion to them . . .

I do not write these words feeling any anger. I can understand and feel for the existing congregation as much as for the rejected youths. It was probably a big mistake to try to introduce that sort of group into that sort of congregation and that sort of building so suddenly. Nevertheless, the story dramatises the problem. The dynamics of a group of people who like each other's company and meet together frequently are not dynamics that assist the outgoingness and change that evangelism calls for.

(This is one of the advantages of the large evangelistic gathering. Groups like the one I mention here would have enjoyed the anonymity of being lost in a crowd. I saw this happen on many occasions in the Mission England stadium meetings.)

What then are the factors in church life that will start off and maintain those relationship processes which account for most people's conversions? I believe there are five elements which need to come together. Those who have the leadership in a congregation need to ensure that progress is being made in each of the five areas.

First, a *church needs to sustain the personal faith of its members*. If individual Christians find their faith exciting and inwardly nourishing, it will show and they will be motivated to pass it on.

Sustaining the personal faith of Christians means that the needs of mind and spirit must be met. This calls for the best that can be offered in terms of teaching ministry and public worship. Many of our most evangelistically-minded clergy fail in these areas. It is all too easy and understandable for a conscientious clergyman to spend so much time visiting and trying to pass on the faith that too little time is left for working out a teaching programme and preparing sermons and other forms of Christian education. I remember being told that a particular photography magazine worked on the policy of ensuring that a regular reader taking copies for a calendar year would have read articles that gave a good grounding in the basics of the hobby.

That seems to me a good example. The regular attender of a particular church, with the will to learn, ought to have a good grasp of Christian basics at the end of that period.

Nor can we simply declare unchallenged truths from pulpits. Christianity is constantly being challenged on television and radio. People are continually facing doubts. Those of us in the ministry are meant to help them face the external and internal challenges to their faith. Either we do it ourselves or we ensure that someone else does it.

Again we often fail when it comes to worship. One of the phenomena of recent British Christianity in the last fifteen years is the rise in the number of events and Christian holidays which centre around 'worship'. Thirty years ago the large evangelical rally never used the word, nor did much about the reality. Now, if anything, we are overbalanced on the other side. But people go to such gatherings in their thousands. They are meeting a need and this can only mean that a large percentage of local congregations offer less satisfying fare.

I believe that teaching without worship which touches the emotions leads to dull Christians. I believe that emotional worship that isn't balanced by teaching that stretches our minds leads to silly Christians! I believe that the local congregation, where people genuinely know each other, is far and away the right context for worship. It is the duty of congregational leaders to work hard so that worship is well planned and sensitively led Sunday by Sunday. This preparation is necessary whether our traditions are liturgical or not. A prayer-book does not take away the need for worship preparation.

But with this desire for worship to be the best we can offer there needs always to be a touch of self-restraint. In a nominally Christian country like the United Kingdom there is always likely to be the uncommitted or seeking attender. We need to express our adoration and our agonising intercession in ways that do not appear ridiculous to the mind of such a person. St Paul was quick to see this (1 Cor. 14:23),

The second necessity for an evangelising church is that *it must support Christian family life*. The second most common route to faith is through the influence of Christian homes. It must therefore be a high priority in any congregational strategy that such homes and families should be helped to do better what they already do well.

Paradoxically, lively churches often have the opposite effects on some of their key households. In 1980, *Family* magazine conducted a survey to discover what were the main pressures felt upon Christian families. The pressure most cited was the demands made by the local church.

It is easy to see how this can happen, especially with regard to membership of small congregations. There is a continued search for leadership for the various activities and ministries. So often one finds that a minority of the members are doing a majority of the work. Sometimes the overworked members actually enjoy being felt indispensable. Many church people find far more satisfaction in the Christian activities than in their Monday-to-Friday jobs. Alas, some people prefer to be doing jobs round at the church than in their homes.

There are far too many church widows and there are too many deserted children.

A great amount of this activity is 'club-church' activity rather than truly missionary and evangelistic. Part of the art of church leadership is not to take on more than the membership can do well. One outstanding Baptist minister known to me, who was put on a new estate to build a new church, saw this clearly. He refused to begin at the 'easy end' with children's Sunday Schools. He could see that the very few adults he had gathered together were not enough to meet the demands of the children and still have time and energy to learn about their Lord and to worship him. Only from the satisfaction of these primary spiritual needs could they do a good job in their own families and among relatives, friends and work-mates. His strategy paid off. The congregation grew until they had the manpower to engage in youth and children's work. Even then he kept Sunday free from these pressures. The 'Sunday School' was on a Tuesday evening in its earliest days.

I can think of several very active church members who got to a point when their only honourable way out of overcommitment was to move house to a new neighbourhood and start again with a new congregation.

Not only must we avoid overloading; we need to give positive help in the task of being Christian parents. This is particularly important for those who are first-generation Christians. The only models for husband and wife that we have are those of our own parents. The only models of father

Churches that Evangelise

and mother that we have are those of our own fathers and mothers.

If a man grows up used to seeing his father out of the house all the time at the pub or fishing or playing golf, then his new-found faith can become an excuse to abandon wife and children in similar fashion for church and other 'Christian' activities. There are many ways in which we need to unlearn what has been picked up from our home backgrounds (although it needs to be said here that such is the reality of 'common grace' and of the Christian influence still present in our society that many 'non-Christian' parents have done a fine job of parenting and deserve our deep thankfulness).

We have to bring up our children in a very different sort of society with different values from the one in which we ourselves were children and adolescents. Parents today need all the help they can get both in terms of teaching and shared experience. The Americans are better at seeing this than the British. The gifted ministry of Dr James Dobson still has no parallel in the United Kingdom. Magazines like *Family* (now renamed *Christian Family*) have a valuable role to play and there are some helpful books in circulation which are written at a popular level.[1]

There is a need to do more in terms of parent groups and possibly occasional parent suppers. Such activities can also have an evangelistic element, for many people begin to think beyond material values when they consider the awesome task of bringing up children.

One of the most helpful things a church can offer the parents in its membership is a well-led youth group. Teenagers are herd animals, bless them! The peer group becomes tremendously important and it is vital for teenagers to catch and share their faith with those of their own generation. This is not always easy. Some inner-city and

[1] The author declares an interest here in that his wife was for some time editor of *Family*.

rural churches can go through patches when they have next to no young people. It is in those situations especially that the camps and house-parties of the Christian national youth organisations are so valuable. Ministers need to know the details and encourage the children of Christian families to go.

A recent development is the rise of the large-scale family camping conventions. Some of these have separate programmes for children and young people and this can be another helpful way of nurturing the young in faith.

The third element required if a church is to encourage natural relational evangelism is that *it needs to sponsor outgoing spirituality*. This is the very opposite of the club mentality.

This outgoing spirituality starts with prayer. A church that has a large place for intercession is more likely to have members who want to do something about the world for which they pray.

In the last decade or so we have seen a growing emphasis on the place of praise and worship. This is healthy as long as it is a balance for intercession, but becomes unhealthy if it crowds out the place for supplication and prayer. There is even an approach to praise and worship which is self-indulgent. It can be great fun to sing praise song after praise song and the tunefulness and the pleasurable experiences can become more important than the person we are praising.

So, then, outgoing spirituality has to be based on casting our cares about the world on to God. But it is hypocritical for most of us to pray about situations and needs that we intend to avoid. Part of a healthy spirituality is a desire and willingness to be involved in the world. Jesus in his famous 'high priestly prayer' did not ask that we should be taken out of the world. Rather his request was for our safety from the evil one (John 17:15).

To be a follower of Jesus is to see the importance of incarnation. It was love for the world that lay behind the

Churches that Evangelise

Lord's incarnation (John 3:16). Our presence in it needs to be from and to reflect the same attitude. The world is full of people made in God's image, exhibiting common grace and facing the same human traumas and joys as we do. A Christianity that pulls its members out of the world all the time will be a false version.

Obviously our employment takes us into the world, but it must not be left at that. I remember visiting a church which had a rule of faith for its members. There were various predictable elements — daily prayer, weekly communion, Bible reading and so forth. Alongside all these requirements was something less predictable — membership of at least one regular activity that would ensure that the church member was involved with people in society at large. Such things as sports and hobbies, clubs and evening classes were mentioned.

But presence in the world needs to be matched with the readiness to speak. The first epistle of Peter contains some good advice. 'Always be prepared to give an answer to everyone who asks you to give the reason for the hope that you have' (1 Pet. 3:15).

The advice goes on to include some wise words about one's demeanour: 'But do this with gentleness and respect, keeping a clear conscience . . .'

Very few of us are called to be preachers — all of us are called to be ready with some answers when asked. Once again the local church can help in this. There are few better group activities than that of people helping each other to describe and sharpen the explanation of the faith that they have.

I have often asked church members to take a piece of paper and sketch out the points that they would like to make in answer to the question: *'What does Christ mean to you?'*

Alongside this readiness to be outgoing and to answer the questions that might come to us about our faith there needs to be an awareness of the network of relationships we all carry. Too much thinking about evangelism is based on the false view that it is something you do to strangers (preferably those you won't meet again). The truth is that in the New Testament era the faith spread through 'households'. Husbands affected wives, and wives their husbands; parents influenced their children; masters spread the faith to their slaves.

Before we encourage new Christians to stand on streetcorners, we need to give them a burden for their families and friends – those within their natural networks of friends and acquaintances. The first Christians were told to share their faith in Jerusalem before they looked at Samaria and 'the ends of the earth' (Acts 1:8). I believe there is sense in that progression and that it works out in our own mini-worlds.

The fourth factor in the creation of an evangelising church is that *it needs to set up 'creation community' occasions*.

Christians belong to two worlds – *the community of the redeemed* and *the community of the created*. Obviously we may feel more at home in the former, but we also belong by right to the latter. Everyone is a creature of God and we share with everyone the pains and pleasures of being human.

There is nothing wrong with churches planning and holding events that have little purpose other than bringing people together to enjoy each other's company in congenial surroundings. By the same token, there is nothing wrong – as I have just been arguing – for Christians to become involved in creating community activities organised by those who do not share the faith.

The danger when a church only confines itself to 'spiritual' activities is that it encourages people to have a compartmentalised attitude to life. It also provides no models (especially to the young) as to how Christians can enjoy themselves together. I am frequently distressed to see that when it comes to holding parties Christian adolescents seem to have no other models for such occasions but those of the world which embody a totally different and sometimes opposed set of values.

I am not arguing for churches running social clubs. What I want to see, and often do, is churches that from time to time pull together their members and their members' friends for times of recreation. Even a parish mission can benefit from a barn dance or barbecue early on and I am *not* thinking that there has to be a mandatory 'preach' to make it respectable.

One particularly important reason for such social activities is that many members of churches are married to people who do not share their faith and feel the pain of divided loyalties. To have occasions where one's 'non-Christian' husband or wife can come, feel at home and find enjoyment can be a real pastoral help to the Christian partner.

In previous years my own church had a vicar who was keen on sailing. Several of our members had sailing-dinghies. On bank-holidays church parties would troop off to the coast with these boats. We would picnic and take turns to sail. We now have Christian men in our congregation who date their conversions back to sitting on the beach on those occasions, having accompanied their wives, and realising that church people were not quite so strange and stuffy as they had supposed.

In many rural communities things are different. There can be such an overlap of the redeemed community and creation community that separately sponsored church activities are unnecessary. What is important is that village fêtes, drama clubs and so on are fully permeated by Christians. We are meant to be salt savouring the whole of society, not simply the parts nearest to the salt-cellar.

The importance of all the factors which I have listed is that if all described was happening in the life of the congregation then Christians would be mingling naturally at all times with those who are unbelievers and seekers and would be better equipped to make their stand for Christ and share their faith. Jesus urged, 'let your light shine before men' (Matt. 5:16). All too often, as a satirical Murray Watts's sketch affirms, Christians can become a fellowship of people who take their light bulbs to a building every Sunday where they all plug in and switch on together!

It is against the background of outgoing members who enjoy and are nourished by their Christianity that any specific evangelistic activities need to be planned. When pastors tell me that some particular approach to evangelism has been tried and found wanting the facts of the matter might well be that any other evangelistic tactic would fail. You cannot harvest if there is no sowing.

This leads me to the final element in the make-up of an evangelising congregation – *it needs to select whom to evangelise*.

Too many efforts at evangelism on the part of churches are haphazard and indiscriminate. I do not see this in the New Testament. St Paul targeted whom he evangelised. His strategy was to go where there was common ground, thus he first made for the synagogue. Only when he was rejected would he switch the bulk of his evangelising energies. Where there was no synagogue, as appears to be the case at Philippi (Acts 16), he went on the Sabbath where people met to pray. In Athens he went to the market-place to trade philosophies with the Epicureans and Stoics. In Ephesus Paul hired a lecture hall and held 'discussions' – doubtless with those whose common ground was more at the 'philosophical' level.

In all this I see Paul either *selecting* his audiences or going about things so that his audiences selected themselves. The common ground was either a search for God or a search for the meaning of life. Paul did not waste his time with those who showed no interest.

Again the Lord himself showed the same selectivity. His message was for those who 'had ears to hear'. When he sent

Churches that Evangelise

out the seventy-two close followers (Matt. 10) his instructions were to go and stay with those who showed openness to them and their message.

In local-church evangelism that should be our basic guideline. Every congregation carries a fringe of people who like to be in contact even if they avoid commitment. In an age when most people live as if God is not particularly important, this desire to keep in contact should be seen as significant and hopeful.

Individual Christians who are open about their faith, should also notice those who like to treat them as friends. It can be a sign of an inner search and in turn a sign of the Holy Spirit's promptings.

What churches need to do is to devise occasions and tactics that will attract and reach those fringes – both the people who keep links with the church as an institution and those who keep links with individual members.

This means, in tactical terms, they either have to reach the fringe people in their own homes, or attract them to centrally-organised meetings or services: or use the 'neutral territory' of people's homes.

Schemes like *Evangelism Explosion*[2] and *Good News Down The Street*[3] have proven track records in terms of reaching people in their own homes. Guest services, large buffet-supper evenings, men's dinners and breakfasts have often proved effective as ways of getting fringers to come at the church's bidding to hear and reflect upon the Gospel.

There is today an increasing use of groups in homes for evangelism. Some approaches start with using Bible passages, others are based on open dicussion and dialogue and some suggest meals with speakers as well as discussion.

---

[2] 228 Shirley Road, Southampton.
[3] See, *Good News Down The Street*, by Michael Wooderson (Grove booklet).

Some churches have trained up leaders to run seekers' groups which can be set up whenever they have contact with five, six or more people who would admit to being in such a condition. One apparently successful church I know bases its whole strategy upon running Christian basics groups. It uses guest services to help both recruit for the groups and complement them.

Most churches that appear to have an evangelistic strategy usually stick to one or two approaches – such as evangelistic visiting or seekers' groups and build their whole strategy around repeating these tactics and continuous improvement of what they are doing. In contrast, some churches which appear to have made little progress can often be found to have thrashed away at just about everything on the market. There is a lesson here.

We need evangelising churches. They, in turn, need evangelising dynamics. To have such they have to make the break from being clubs for Christians and for those who like things the way they are. It is a painful break to make. It challenges some long-held traditions – yes and many of the new fashions also. Archbishop William Temple was surely right when he said, 'The Christian Church is the one organisation in the world that exists purely for the benefit of non-members.'

The New Testament teaching that the Church is the body of Christ has been much emphasised in the last fifteen years. It has been a healthy corrective to excessive individualism and private piety.

However, the first body of Christ – Jesus himself – spent no time glorying in his arms and legs and wondering whether they were correctly balanced and linked. He *used* his body to *go* from place to place, to teach his message and to die for others. In the same way the congregation which glories in being the body of Christ must see this description not in static but in dynamic terms. We are meant to give Christ the ability to keep *going* and to keep teaching and even in a sense to keep suffering and dying for others (Col. 1:24).

Only when this sort of unselfishness is reflected in the life style of a congregation can we expect to see effective evangelism happening.

9
Preaching for a Verdict

A few years ago I became conscious of having 'lost' something in my own preaching as an evangelist. While I was not in the 'big league' as an evangelist and used to seeing scores of people flooding forward to respond to Christ as a result of my sermons, I nevertheless felt that there should be more 'fruit' from my attempts to preach the Gospel.

There had been times in the past when more had responded. Somehow such responses were becoming rare.

At this point I have to say that evangelism is far more than head counting after sermons. However, the essential gift of an evangelist is a gift to arouse faith in unbelievers and this is bound to become obvious in people's lives and therefore measurable.

The effectiveness of an evangelistic speaker is related to a complex number of factors and not all of these can be pinned down. One of the factors is, however, very easy to pin down. If there is next to nobody in the audience who needs converting it is hardly likely that there will be much by way of 'results'! In a great many British evangelistic services and meetings the percentage of unbelievers and seekers present is tiny.

I have come to believe that there is a link between the amount of prayer and the obvious results in set-piece evangelism. I believe this was probably the key factor in

Mission England where such a remarkably high proportion of people responded to Billy Graham's preaching.

At the end of the day we cannot organise the Holy Spirit or know all the purposes of God in any given situation. All the evangelistic preacher can do is to tell the story and urge his listeners to take it seriously. Nevertheless, there are some lessons to be learned and when I was going through my time of 'poor results' I decided to send myself back to school. I went to listen to the person who I feel is one of the best evangelists in Britain – a vicar called John Collins, who probably taught his curate, the late David Watson, just about everything he knew.

I sat listening to John when he was preaching on a mission, and I made notes – not of *what* he said but about the way he said it. Soon afterwards I had to preach at an evangelistic service. I opened my notes as I prepared my new sermon. I went and preached with the lessons learnt built into my approach. There was a remarkable response as a result.

In this chapter I want to share some of the lessons I have learnt about evangelistic preaching. None of what I shall write is original – it is all borrowed! For some years I have stumped around the country trying to teach pastors and teachers how to preach the Gospel in such a way that people will respond. It has been gratifying to receive letters and to be told by those who have listened to me on the subject how they, too, have seen 'results' once they started preaching in a way that embodied some of the lessons that I have learnt.

I believe that while there is a particular *gift* of an evangelist it is still possible for others without such a gift to preach in such a way that people come to belief. Again, while I do not believe that techniques are the secret of evangelistic preaching, I have come to see that there are particular considerations which help us to be more effective when trying to present the Gospel.

I also believe that the churches of Britain need to hear

more and better evangelistic sermons. They not only can result in conversions among the unsure who come to church; they dramatise an agenda that all who hear can sense is vital and this in turn helps in their own attitude to witnessing and faith-sharing.

First we need to be clear about what we are trying to do in an evangelistic sermon. There are four tasks it must achieve.

It must *proclaim*. The whole Gospel is too big for any one sermon, but you cannot preach the Gospel without spelling out some of the basic truths that centre on the person of Christ – what he taught, why he died, the significance of his resurrection and his ability to come to us now through the Holy Spirit.

It must persuade. An evangelistic sermon is not about the detached consideration of certain matters that are of interest. It is about persuading people to reject their false gods and false securities and to embrace the truth. 'Since, then, we know what it is to fear the Lord, we try to persuade men', wrote Paul the Apostle (2 Cor. 5:11). Perhaps the outstanding quality of Billy Graham's preaching is this note of persuasion.

It must be personal. There is no way an evangelistic sermon can be detached and talk about *the* Gospel. It must carry the flavour of Paul's little phrase – '*my* gospel' (Rom. 2:16). If Jesus Christ is good news and life-changing then the hearer has a right to feel that the preacher has 'tried the product' and is 'a satisfied customer'.

It must be practical. When Peter preached his famous sermon on the day of Pentecost the crowds began to ask: 'Brothers, what shall we do?' (Acts 2:37). Peter gave a specific and practical answer to that specific question and he was not afraid to claim that if the steps he called for were taken then, without a doubt, sins would be forgiven and the Spirit would be received.

The call to take practical steps and the courage to affirm

that those who take such steps will be forgiven by God and receive his Holy Spirit is at the heart of an evangelistic sermon.

One doesn't need to have a particular gift from God to bear these considerations in mind when preparing a sermon which one hopes will help people to put their faith in Christ.

It is also helpful, when preparing, to reflect upon the thoughts and feelings of those who will be listening. One of the fashionable things to say is that our evangelism must be contextualised. That means, according to some, that we must pronounce on unemployment, social deprivation, global injustice and other aspects of the world around us.

This is, in my judgment, a mistake, but a good mistake to make! If God is righteous then those who represent him must not give the impression that he is neutral on those aspects of life where people – *his creatures* – get hurt. Further, the call to discipleship is a call to live and work in such a way that God's righteousness and love are reflected wherever we have influence.

Having said this, it can be disastrous to centre a Gospel sermon on matters like unemployment and poverty. Far too many people, alas, live in a way that keeps them from thinking about the hurts around them. Their souls are not touched by these matters. They ought to be, but they are not. There is also the danger that dogmatic talk in these areas will stir up what, in communication jargon, is called 'noise'. The hearers will stop listening having branded us as 'political'.

We also need to be clear that many of the social and political matters that affect our context are extremely complex and do not admit of simple dogmatic answers. I have no doubt that Christians are meant to be in the forum wrestling with political and social matters, unafraid to speak prophetically and judgmentally; but in an evangelistic sermon we have to meet people where they are and offer the life-changing grace of God which often leads to radical changes of moral and social stance in the convert. Zacchaeus was a swindling tax-collector and traitor. When Jesus met him he did not talk about his crooked ways. He offered Zacchaeus an encounter with the very presence of God. The result was repentance and restitution. Jesus never, as far as we can see, brought up the subject of his wicked ways, but that encounter with Jesus helped Zacchaeus to realise how wicked he was (Luke 19).

The task of the evangelist is to help similar encounters to take place. He or she must speak so that people 'see Jesus'. But the evangelist is in the introductions business. Once a person is in the fellowship of Christ and his people, that person will discover that he or she is one of a community whose life and words are meant to judge the world and its values.

In all this I am not saying that the evangelist is meant to be a deceiver. The evangelistic sermon is not a smooth sales-pitch concealing the full cost of the product. There is, however, always the danger that the product cannot be seen because people's attention is pulled into too many other valid but not central areas. When one is spelling out repentance and the Lordship of Christ, the preacher can and must give indicators of the cost and the challenge of Christianity.

Thus far I have spoken about preaching the Gospel in the light of social and political contexts which affect but do not hurt the hearer. It is different when the contexts do cause hurt. Raymond Fung, Secretary of Evangelism with the World Council of Churches, has argued that for many people who are hurt by their social and political contexts, their experience of human sin is more from being sinned-against than sinning. I believe this is the case and that evangelistic preaching to such groups needs to show that God is not on the side of the oppressors. But we must not be naïve about human nature. We speak of a God who loves sinners as well as the sinned-against. We need to beware of the many

Preaching for a Verdict

political forces who come to the sinned-against communities posing as champions, but with a message of resentment and hate. The Gospel must not be confused with such a message.

The context that must not be ignored, however, is the basic humanness of every hearer. The Gospel has a redeeming message for all men and women. We most certainly must preach the Gospel in a contextualised way with regard to humanness.

Billy Graham frequently mentions the five assumptions about his hearers which he makes when he is preparing a sermon. I shall simply list them without comment.

1. People are aware that they have needs that are not being met by social improvement or affluence.
2. There is an essential 'emptiness' in every life without Christ.
3. People experience frequently a sense of loneliness.
4. People have a sense of guilt.
5. There is a universal fear of death.

What, then, are some of the things that need to be borne in mind in preaching the Gospel?

The first consideration is that the end of the sermon is the business end. If the sermon starts too late or if the preacher takes too long to get to the invitation to respond then effectiveness will suffer as the hearers' alertness will be impaired. I have seen Billy Graham become visibly anxious when the service or meeting where he is preaching drags on. On one occasion when the sermon was being delayed and when I tried to reassure him he replied, 'That's all very well, but these people are going to be tired.'

The invitation takes time to make, explain and conduct. It needs at least ten minutes. To hurry it is to present repentance and faith as afterthoughts.

The second consideration is that the invitation must not be 'sprung' upon the hearers. Again it is interesting to note that Billy Graham often indicates within the very early sentences of his sermons that he intends to call for a response. In his case it seems hardly necessary. It is common knowledge that he asks hearers to 'get up out of their seats'. With preachers who do not normally do this sort of thing there needs to be an early mention of the fact that the invitation is coming.

The third consideration is that the preacher has to realise that he or she cannot cover all the Gospel. There has to be a narrowing-down of the ground covered. I personally believe, however, that there has to be a clear link between the ground covered and the cruciality of the Cross. That link needs to be revealed even if the basic message of any particular sermon is not about the Cross.

The fourth consideration is that the hearer needs to be convinced of the relevance of what is being proclaimed to the world that he or she considers to be the real world. There has to be application. There has to be a reaction in the hearer that leads to the thought, 'This preacher knows what my life is all about and this message relates to it!'

One of the best ways to reveal the relevance of Christ and his Gospel is to expose the folly of trying to live without him. Jeremiah was commissioned by God 'to uproot and tear down, to destroy and overthrow', as well as 'to build and to plant' (Jer. 1:10). If people are to see the goodness of the good news they must be helped to see the bleakness and the bad news of the substitutes in which they may be trusting.

On that particular day when I sat, notebook in hand, listening to John Collins I learnt a valuable lesson on this. Rather than making a series of statements condemning the folly of life without Christ, he asked a series of probing questions about the wisdom of such a way of life. He *interrogated* his hearers. On reflection I can see how much Jesus himself used questions in his preaching and personal discussions.

If an assertion with which I disagree is made at me from the pulpit the chances are that I shall be hardened in my disagreement. If I have – and this is at the heart of being a sinner – a rebellious inner attitude towards God then I won't like being told how much I am in the wrong.

If on the other hand someone who seems to exude a spirit of love and concern gently questions the things I am taking for granted or avoiding to face then there is far more of a chance that I shall respond by reviewing thoughtfully what is being questioned. And the powerful thing about such a process of induced reflection is that, as a result of responding to the questions, *I shall see something for myself*. It is not that I simply 'swallow' what I am being told, *I shall have made a discovery*. Good preaching is an interactive exercise in which the preacher helps his or her listeners to make discoveries.

But to say this about the use of questions implies something. If one asks a question, one needs to give time for an answer. This is true in two-way discussions, but it is also true when the question is rhetorical. Listening to John Collins on that morning when I went to hear him preach, I noticed that although he was under pressure of time he still allowed pauses for people to reflect on his carefully-framed questions. He had the courage to stop filling the air with his words and allow the pressure of silence to make us search for answers in our own hearts.

If preachers could only learn that one lesson well it would make a remarkable difference to their pulpit efforts.

Not only must the preacher expose the actual irrelevance of all the false gospels; he or she needs to work in and rub home the relevance and goodness of what is being offered as the answer.

It is here that I also learnt something valuable from listening to John Collins. His way of handling this part of his task was again not so much to make assertions but to tell stories. He spoke of people he knew, ordinary people with whom his listeners could identify. He told us how Christ had changed their lives.

John Mallison, an Australian evangelist and teacher who has become a good friend, actually goes one better than telling other people's stories. On occasions he will bring the people concerned with him to testify in their own words. This might not seem particularly novel. Testimonies are a common element in evangelistic services and meetings. What is novel about John Mallison's approach is that he incorporates the testimonies *into* the sermon.

(David Watson had another way of doing this sort of thing. He would incorporate small sketches, often humorous, into his sermons. Sometimes it seemed that he was not so much preaching as compèring his sermons using sketches and even a song to be part of his presentations of the Gospel. It could be an extremely effective way of proceeding, although drama could be lost if one was trying to preach to a huge crowd in a large stadium.)

The fifth consideration in evangelistic preaching is that the hearers need to be given a procedure that will help them to know that they have responded to the Gospel. Dr R. T. Kendall has written at length on this in his book, *Stand up and be Counted*.[1]

This aspect of evangelistic preaching is open to abuse. Some feel strongly there is always the danger that a crude head-counting exercise can take place and that the preacher is under pressure to get people standing up or going forward to prove his worth. This pressure on the preacher is transferred into a pressure on the congregation.

The mind boggles at what could be done. Soft music, beguiling choirs, frightening warnings of coming hell and so on. I must live in a sheltered world, for I have not actually encountered any of these horrors. If I did I should condemn such abuses.

---

[1] Hodder & Stoughton (1984).

Preaching for a Verdict

What I have felt uneasy about is where preachers have so widened the invitation that it is almost impossible *not* to stand or go forward. The appeal is not so much to turn from darkness to light, but a play upon the poverty of one's discipleship and a call for those who want 'to follow more closely' or 'to be filled with more of his Spirit', or if they have been convicted about some area of their life, 'to come forward and seek "ministry"'.

I should want to say that I do not recognise such appeals as having anything to do with genuine Gospel preaching. They suggest to me a preacher or a group of meeting organisers who want to be gratified rather than an attempt to help people who want to respond to the love of God.

In the appeal or invitation the preacher is acting as a spiritual midwife. He or she is there to assist a clean start to a new life. It is the Spirit who brings people to Christ and makes them children of the heavenly Father. That same Spirit needs our voice-boxes to explain to those who want to say 'yes' to Christ how to do it. And those same voice-boxes can give words of assurance when the response has been made.

In the invitation the preacher is not trying to force people to do what they don't want to do. He or she is trying to help them to do what they *do* want to do. The line on this matter must never be crossed.

The actual ways of conducting an invitation can vary, but whatever pattern is used two things are always necessary. The first is that it must not be hurried. The second is that *the hearer is called to move beyond making a resolution in his thought life.* There must be an accompanying piece of body language.

This sort of thinking is enshrined in the sacraments where we talk about outward signs of inward intentions. There is no culture known to me that recognises as valid a marriage that is nothing more than two people mentally deciding to marry.

There needs to be some demonstrating action. This can have a public purpose – and in marriage one can immediately see the social value of the open activity. It can also, however, have great private and personal value.

Every day myriads of thoughts flit through our minds. When does a passing thought become a permanent intention? I can flick through the pages of a photographic magazine and entertain passing thoughts about owning some new, gadget-riddled camera. Not until my body takes me out of the door and moving towards the shop has my life been changed.

In the middle of a busy life I might well have a passing thought that it would be nice to phone up a long-lost friend. Not until I reach for the phone or at least scribble a reminder note in my diary is there any chance that the thought that is here today will not be gone tomorrow.

The marriage of bodily action to thought is part of what it means to be an integrated person. The last thing we should wish to encourage is a disintegrated Christianity. There are already far too many people who live as Christians in terms of their mental agendas yet are sub-Christian in their outer lives. We do not want to recruit any more to the already swollen ranks of private Christians.

Doug Barnett, the winsome and witty evangelist with the Saltmine Trust, put it well on one occasion when I heard him. 'You cannot be a secret disciple. Either the secrecy will end the discipleship or the discipleship will end the secrecy.'

This plea for a response of mind and body does *not* mean that any particular way of doing it has to be canonised. In a large auditorium it makes a great deal of sense to ask people to 'get up out of their seats' and come forward. How else can they be identified and given further help? What needs to be remembered, however, is that there is a certain comforting anonymity in walking forward amid thousands of people. To

Preaching for a Verdict 131

be asked to do it in a village church in front of eighteen other people who all know you is something quite different and much harder.

Marney Patterson, the Canadian evangelist who is an Anglican minister, has an interesting and well-conceived approach to the invitation. On every seat in the building where he is conducting a meeting there is a simple, multiple-choice decision card with a tear-off section. A small pencil is fitted into slots in the card.

At the end of his sermon Patterson will spell out the decision that needs to be made. He then calls the congregation to a time of silence and reflection for some two minutes. I have begun to use this time of silence in my invitation procedure and find it powerful and effective.

When the congregation has considered its response in silence, Patterson invites them to pick up the card and pencil, fill in their names and then enter their response by ticking the appropriate box on the card. He couples this suggestion with a careful explanation of the implications of a first-time commitment or a rededication. He includes two more possible responses – both unselfish. The respondent may indicate a desire to offer for full-time service in the church at large or, alternatively, for service in his or her home congregation.

When time has been given to complete the cards Patterson suggests that those who have made a response tear off the take-home section of the card which contains some simple guidelines for Christian growth. These can be put in pockets or handbags.

There is then a hymn and during the hymn there is an 'offering'. All who have filled up a card are invited during the hymn to come forward and to place the completed card in an offertory plate as their personal offering to Christ. By remaining forward they can then be counselled.

In the best sense of the word it is all rather 'churchy',

which fits in well with the atmosphere in some Anglican churches and cathedrals.

My personal preference is to lead up to a simple prayer of commitment which I say slowly on behalf of those present who feel they want to take a step of faith. This is what I saw John Collins doing on that day when I went to study his preaching. Before leading the prayer he was careful to explain that it was only for those who genuinely felt God's Spirit calling them to do so.

Before I lead the prayer of commitment (inviting respondents to echo the prayer in their own minds), I give advance notice that at the end of the meeting I want those who pray to come up to tell me and to be given a follow-up leaflet. I then pray something along these lines:

Dear Father, I admit that I have been in the wrong with you and that I need to be put right and forgiven.

Thank you for loving me and sending Jesus to show me your love and to die, in my place, for my sins.

And now I'm saying YES to you! I want to follow the way of Jesus. I want you to be my personal heavenly Father.

I ask that your Holy Spirit will come into my life and help me to know you and change me to be more like you want me to be . . . and help me to serve you for the rest of my life! Amen

To insist upon a bodily response so that the respondent can be identified is essential to the spiritual midwifery. When people come up to me after praying the prayer (usually after the formal closure of the meeting), I am able to get a note of name and address and to find out if there is any immediate misunderstanding or blockage. Billy Graham is right to call such people 'enquirers' rather than 'converts'. Very often there is much pastoral work to be done in the weeks to come to ensure a clean and completely experienced 'new birth'. To leave it at the level of people's private thoughts is to invite the building-up of confusions and, in some cases, subsequent disillusion.

At this point we must face a very serious objection about evangelistic appeals and invitations. Is it possible they can encourage a sort of 'decisionism'? Can they lead to people saying 'I've done the deed that makes me a Christian so I'm saved!' Those Christians who fear this take the view that it is the choice of God and not the choice of men and women that decides who is 'saved'. I happen to agree with the basic theological standpoint from which this criticism comes. I believe, however, that the danger of encouraging people to see the invitation as a sort of saving work is greatly exaggerated.

Much depends on how the preacher explains the invitation. I have never heard any evangelist claim that 'coming forward will save them'. Indeed, I have frequently heard Billy Graham say precisely the opposite.

Again it is important that the response to the invitation is seen in exactly those terms – *response* to an *invitation*. A true Gospel sermon should centre not on what *we* have to do but on what God has done and is able to do in the present and future. It should carry the strong fragrance of grace and not demand. This is not always an easy balance to maintain when one is also trying to undermine the false securities which keep people from seeing the wonder of God's love.

The final consideration of evangelistic preaching is that one must take responsibility for all who make a response. I have already written about the aspect of spiritual midwifery. If we extend the analogy we can see that newborn (or perhaps in many cases, half-born) babes cannot be left to fend for themselves. The evangelistic preacher needs to show a concern for those who respond. Keith de Berry, who is supposed to be a retired Church of England rector, but who is an astonishingly active evangelist, always tries to send a personal letter to every person who makes a response at his meetings and services.

But the evangelist's main responsibility at this point is to effect a smooth transfer of the enquirer and his concerns to those with pastoral oversight in the local church. In the case of an evangelistic service held in or by the local church this transfer should be relatively simple, but the point to bear in mind is the need for supportive counselling and friendship over the first couple of months. In Mission England we found the role of a nurture group at this stage to be of great value.

This book attempts to look at the big picture of evangelising a nation. Why then a chapter on preaching the Gospel in the local church?

I believe that a nominal Christian context such as one finds in many parts of the United Kingdom means that there are usually many uncommitted people in our pews or within easy reach of a local-church evangelistic service. If our pastors attempted to preach for a verdict more often there would be many pleasant surprises.

The very fact that we were doing this would dramatise the agenda of evangelism to the congregation, and I believe it would stimulate more natural day-by-day congregational desire to share the Gospel. It may be a tiny step, but as some ancient Chinese sage is supposed to have said one day: 'The journey of a thousand miles begins with a single step!'

10

Electronic Gospel?

When the BBC presented a Billy Graham meeting from Birmingham on television in 1984 there were 7,000 letters, mostly asking for counselling material.

When Ian Knox, my colleague at the Church Pastoral Aid Society, was televised preaching a simple Gospel sermon from a parish church one Sunday a year later, over 1,500 people out of a much smaller viewing audience wrote in to indicate some sort of response.

The question has to be put: Could we evangelise the nation via television?

At this point some realities have to be faced. In the United Kingdom there is a total commitment to public-service broadcasting. On the one hand the government is kept at arm's length and on the other individual groups cannot buy time. The BBC and the companies who win the IBA franchises have to work to strictly monitored codes which are conceived to be in the public interest. There are particular ways that this affects religion.

Both the broadcasting authorities are committed to maintaining a religious (not only Christian) output. This means that a basic minimum of programming – much of it to extremely high standards – is set aside each week. Although there is not so clearly defined a 'closed period' on Sundays as there used to be, there is still a degree of collusion between the authorities to avoid a religious programme (which is assumed to be of minority interest) having to compete on one channel with something of extremely high viewing potential on the other.

Although Christianity does not have the field to itself, it does have the lion's share of available time. The value to the churches of the time given to Christian programmes must equal millions of pounds. The question is, however, are the programmes made and transmitted the ones which the churches would want to put out if they were buying the time?

The answer has to be – *no*.

Many evangelical and other highly-committed theologically conservative groups are extremely dissatisfied with the present situation. They want to see programmes made that proclaim and argue for the Gospel. They want to reach millions for Christ and they believe that television and radio can do it. Some of them point to the United States where Christian groups can buy time to air the sorts of programmes they want and where there are even Christian stations and channels.

Evangelists such as Jerry Falwell, they argue, have nationwide ministries and even have a bearing on who gets elected president.

At this point, however, the enthusiasts fall foul of the whole philosophy of public-service broadcasting. Setting aside for the moment whether television and radio can be effective in winning people to the faith, should Christians have the right to expect it to be used in this manner? Dr Colin Morris, the head of BBC Religious Broadcasting Department, has grappled with this and other issues in his book *God-in-a-Box*.[1] Here is his conclusion:

> How can the religious output of a public service broadcasting organisation and the response of the churches be

[1] Hodder & Stoughton (1984).

synchronized without a privileged relationship being set up which the BBC's Charter or the IBA's Act of Parliament would outlaw? . . . religious television has no mandate to recruit viewers to a lifetime vocation in the service of the truth it conveys.[1]

Public-service broadcasting cannot allow itself to be 'used' by sections of the Church to preach to the masses. For one reason why should this evangelising use stop at evangelical Christianity? Why not preach Islam or Buddhism or Mormonism? Why stop at religion? Why not hand over the airwaves to Marxists or Fascists to preach their message?

But there is another reason. Evangelical Christianity is not the only version available and, as I said in an earlier chapter, it is still a minority group within a minority group within the nation. It is hard to see why we Christians who want to reach the nation should expect any favours.

In the apportionment of time and programming, the broadcasting authorities have to reflect the various traditions which exist. This needs to be understood because many zealous Christians are convinced that humanists and atheists plot away in religious broadcasting to keep the simple Gospel away from the public.

The truth is that over the past five decades Christianity has lost its hold on the population and other faiths have entered the scene with the various immigrant groupings. The religious programming of a public-service system has to reflect the changing position. If we want to see positive, orthodox, affirmative Christian programmes, then the situation on the ground has to be dominated by these characteristics.

It is not.

This is not to say that I would defend the entire record of

[1] Ibid. p. 128

the two authorities regarding religious broadcasting. I think that the pressures to be entertaining or 'newsy', plus the personal stances of some of the advisers and producers, have affected the output. I share the view that evangelical and Catholic Christians are not seen at their best. I believe that the perceived 'coolness' of the medium means that the *searcher* gets more coverage than the *finder*. I think that too little attempt has been made to find and promote attractive, enthusiastic, popular advocates of the faith. In other areas of broadcasting we have Patrick Moore sharing his enthusiasm for astronomy and David Bellamy romping through programmes about botany with an infectious sense of fun. When it comes to Christianity the presenters are often apparently neutral and cool.

Having said this, and supposing my contention is right, whom should we blame? Do we expect the religious departments of public-service broadcasting companies to go talent spotting among the churches?

I know from my years of service on the Central Religious Advisory Committee for the BBC and IBA that while those departments do indeed try to keep their eyes open, there is also a place for private enterprise. There has in recent years been much criticism of the amount of exposure given to the Rev. Don Cupitt on the BBC. He has been given the longest-ever religious programme and has presented two very lavishly produced TV series – both very destructive of the orthodox Christian position.

Is this evidence of subtle plots against the Gospel in high places? I don't think so. Quite simply, Don Cupitt is a very good broadcaster who comes up with some very televisable ideas. It probably helps that he is unorthodox in his views as this gives his programmes the added relish of being 'daring' and different – which might help the ratings.

Evangelicals have, I believe, a particular problem. Our ablest communicators are, generally, *preachers*. Radio and television are more intimate forms of communication according to the accepted wisdom on the matter. The electronic communicator is someone in a small room chatting casually rather than in some great auditorium proclaiming formally.

While I believe there are effective ways of televising the proclaimer, I have to agree with the accepted wisdom. But one can go further still. Television is about pictures, images, moods. It needs pictures as well as, perhaps *more* than, words. The traditional Christian modes of communication are words – spoken and written. A small screen with one talking head on it is, after a short while, boring except to someone already in strong sympathy with either the head or the words.

Television calls for drama and the use of the visual arts. Evangelical Christians have, until recently, had all too little a place for such modes of expression. And when recourse has been made to drama in so-called 'Christian films' there has been a tendency to ask the dramatist to produce visual tracts which have little feel for the complexities of personalities or life in general.

Through the skills of a new wave of writers such as Murray Watts, I believe we are seeing remarkable changes in these fields, but the after-effects of a certain artistic barrenness are still with us.

We now come to a totally new factor – technological progress. The situation I have outlined is one where a public-service 'duopoly' dominates British broadcasting. Together they provide the only electronic publishing houses available. In the world of book publishing there are hundreds of outlets and one can even try to publish and distribute one's own efforts. In radio and television this is impossible (apart from one or two pirate radio stations). Tremendous power to influence what the nation perceives to be the truth about the religious situation is in the hands of a very few people.

The days of this duopoly, however, could well be numbered. For some time there has been government encouragement for the development of cable networks which could, in effect, bring more electronic publishers into business, albeit in localised settings. More significant still is the emergence of the Direct Broadcasting Satellite (DBS). There are already several of these in place and through them a new range of channels could be opened up for the viewer – perhaps through link-ups to the developing cable networks or through individual receiving dishes fitted to people's houses.

The implications of this new technology for highly-motivated Christian groups are obvious. If the public-service giants control and inhibit what various groups want to say, could they get in through the back door of the DBS and cable? Already it is known that American television evangelists are looking with interest at the United Kingdom and waiting to move in. Already there are certain British groups making programmes for the now available (if strictly limited) DBS and cable opportunities.

I am confident that this developing technology will break the public-service duopoly. The future British public will have more choice. There will be more electronic publishing houses and we shall see the development of directly evangelistic programmes.

What I confess to being unsure about is whether this will be a good thing! Anyone who has watched some of the American programmes with their show-biz presentation and their appeals for money must, at least, have mixed feelings about the prospect. Such programmes are light years away from the broadcast of the Birmingham Billy Graham meeting that I mentioned at the beginning of this chapter.

I fear that the increasing choice could very well be a choice out of a set of almost identical alternatives. But if this would genuinely 'reach the masses' it would be worth it. My second fear, however, is that a rash of future satellite and cable programmes would actually diminish the impact of Christianity in the nation.

In the USA – according to research done by Peter Horsfield – only some 24 per cent of the adult population watch an hour or so of religious television a week. That is only about a half of the number of people who – on some estimates – go to church on a Sunday!

Of course we are talking about 24 per cent of a much larger population than we have in the United Kingdom. This means that there is a great deal of money available as a result of appeals for funds. Horsfield's research, however, hardly presents much assurance that if the UK was to develop a range of American-style programmes then vast numbers would be reached. Indeed, it would appear that a higher percentage of people watch religious programmes in the UK than in the USA, in spite of (or because of) the public-service detached approach.[3]

There is, however, something even more disturbing about the American situation. The rise of independently-financed evangelical programmes on the minor networks has led to the demise of religious programming on the great national networks. The vast majority of American viewers stay tuned to the national networks, but the religious programming is now concentrated on the smaller and more localised outlets. In relative terms, what we have in the USA, is 'narrowcasting' the Gospel rather than 'broadcasting'.

We need to be clear about one basic matter. The fact that the Gospel is widely available does not mean that people want to hear it. We have churches open all over the country every week, but only a minority go in through their doors. Why should we assume that people who are not motivated to go to church on a Sunday will be more motivated to search out some minority interest channel and tune into Gospel

[3] According to David Winter of the BBC, the percentage of the UK population watching religious TV every week stands at 29.

programmes? The sky could be full of satellites beaming down evangelistic programmes that very few are bothering to watch.

Of course, the Christians may well watch. They will be asked to support such programmes financially. That means that what Christian groups want and enjoy will be what gets the money. It may well not be what is needed to make an impact on the non-Christian viewer.

And all the time the pressure could be on the public-service authorities to phase out religious programmes because the need is being met elsewhere. The American experience suggests that this will happen. The chances are that a move into DBS and cable (assuming changes in the law to allow such developments) will marginalise the Gospel rather than evangelise the nation.

I still believe that the best strategy is for the churches to encourage young people with Christian commitment into the media. We want more people pursuing excellence in religious broadcasting through the genuinely *broad*-casting agencies. We need to make sure that those who produce religious programmes are better advised as to the strength of interest in religion generally and the growing number of effective contemporary communicators that are being thrown up in the present situation.

I do not believe we should be leaping into the new opportunities that technology will create. However, we cannot ignore them either. I believe it is inevitable that the public-service duopoly will break down and that more choice and more electronic publishers will have their place in the sun. As that happens I want to see highly-professional trained communicators and programme-makers who have earned their spurs in the major networks branching out into the new channels with eminently watchable, sensitive and entertaining programmes.

One question remains. If I were to get my way would that

Electronic Gospel?

lead to reaching the nation for Christ? I fear the answer is 'no'. We still have to face the fact that the vast majority of people in this country choose to be uncommitted. You are not meeting such people 'where they are' by expecting them voluntarily to choose to watch programmes calling them to commitment.

Jesus recognised this problem by speaking in parables when he also recognised that most people in the crowds around him did not have 'ears to hear'. We need to explore the television equivalent of parable and it may well be that the answers lie in drama, documentary and music.

'What – someone might well ask – about the points made at the opening of this chapter? Did not thousands write in for literature as a result of those transmissions of sermons by Billy Graham and Ian Knox?' Yes. What we do not know, however, is whether that response would be repeated if the same sort of programme were done every week.

My feeling is that the authorities ought, as a public service, to give more time to those sorts of events and speakers. They command more support and generate more interest on the ground than any skilful deviser and presenter of destructive, radical religious programmes. Having said this, I feel that 'reaping' activities are not the best use of radio and television. The problem of providing nurture and links into Christian fellowships is far more acute with radio and television than with any large evangelistic mission.

In every sense of the word, Christians are meant to be in touch with each other.

The proper use of radio and television is more to do with 'sowing' than 'reaping'. I believe that the general public needs to see what Christians are doing and saying. We need programmes that challenge today's false gospels and trigger off the search for Christ. We need to encounter men and women locked into attractive certainties about God – whether they are presenting or being presented. We need to see human and informal aspects of Christian congregations as well as those congregations at formal worship. Yes – and we need to be shown that worship can be the joyous and relaxed activity of very normal people. The public has a right to know, for example, that thousands of youthful people gather frequently to worship God in contemporary and exuberant ways. The sedate and well-ordered Sunday Service from the average 'mainline' church does not tell the half of what is happening in the Christian world today!

We need to see men and women of Christian convictions who have taken their faith into sport, business, politics and the social services, and, indeed, all areas of life. What difference has their faith made? What makes them 'tick' as human beings? What are their goals?

It is against this background that straight calls to discipleship – whether on radio and television or in other contexts – are more likely to be effective. The danger of a diet of unremitting evangelistic programmes is that people have so little notion of what the call is *to*. Christianity can too easily become just another compartment in a world full of compartments which have no necessary connections.

What some British Christians find attractive about American religious television is not so much the creativity or content of the programmes, as the *commitment* of the participants. It is here that I find the British public-service broadcasting approach to be at its weakest.

Lady Plowden – in my hearing – once put her finger on the problem. 'Why is it,' she said, 'that when I watch a sports programme I feel that the commentators are trying to convert me to the sport, but when I watch a religious programme, I don't get that same feeling?'

Too often our British programmes are presented with a detachment that drains some of the impact from the content. This is not always the case, admittedly. When Don Cupitt is given the freedom of the small screen to present his radical understandings, he comes over with some real impact. Alas orthodoxy does not have such champions or such budgets (although Keith Ward has shown through radio, that such champions are in existence).

I do *not* believe, however, that there is a conspiracy against orthodoxy or even evangelism in the public-service system. A large part of the blame must rest with evangelical Christians, who have waited too long for 'them to do something about it' when they should have encouraged creativity in their own ranks and come up with good ideas and concepts.

The situation is, I believe, improving. That is why I fear that a change in legislation and technology, and the flooding in of American or American-style programmes could do more harm than good for the cause of the Gospel. It would be tragic if the major British networks were to follow the example of their US counterparts and retreat from making religious programmes, leaving it to the enthusiasts with money to spend on the much smaller cable and satellite outlets.

The nation will not be 'reached' through Christian radio and TV any more than the nation has been reached through Christian publishing houses.

The lessons from the world of books need to be learnt. In the UK we have some very creative Christian publishing companies (I am proud to be associated with one of them). We have a growing number of enthusiastically-run Christian bookshops. What happens, however, is that most of these publishers target their product where they know it will sell, which is in the already committed Christian sector of society. The channel to that sector is, mainly, the bookshops specialising in Christian books and Bibles. Where a town has an effective Christian bookshop the chances are that the local secular bookshop will not stock any Christian books – or at least only those few with a clear appeal to the uncommitted such as a book by pop-singer Cliff Richard, or children's Bible stories.

Very few Christian books get into the great chain operators like W. H. Smith. Thus, for all the increased expertise of the publishers and undoubted commitment in the product, the nation is not being reached through Christian literature. Non-Christians who read such books usually do so through being given copies by believing friends.

I fear that the same dynamics will happen in any brave new world of 'Christian broadcasting'. In fact the people of Britain can already hear evangelists like Billy Graham and Dick Saunders every week. They broadcast on relatively unknown wavelengths coming in from commercial European stations. How many actually know about this? My guess is that the bulk of the listening audiences to such programmes already has a commitment to the faith, otherwise they would not seek out the particular stations and programmes.

Before enthusiastic advocates persuade us to reach for our cheque-books and finance the brave new age of Christian radio and television companies, we need to think very carefully. For me, with some reluctance, the conclusion is clear. In the task of reaching the nation for Christ there is no electronic short cut.

11
Words, Works and Wonders

At the heart of evangelism there is a message. There is no escaping that fact.

It is true that the majority of converts come into a relationship with Christ because it was 'caught rather than taught', but that does not alter the fact that there is a clear message – a story to tell which is good news.

The New Testament bears this out using terms like 'Gospel' (good news) and 'word'. Jesus in himself is the ultimate 'Word' (John 1), but Paul would write about 'the word of God' (2 Cor. 4:2), the 'word of life' (Phil. 2:16) and the 'word of Christ' (Col. 3:16).

When the first Christian community was under stress and attempted to get itself better organised, the leaders were clear that while the organisation of compassion had to be done, and done well, their first priority was to give themselves 'to prayer and the ministry of the word' (Acts 6:4).

When persecution broke up the church in Jerusalem we read: 'Those who had been scattered *preached the word* wherever they went. Philip went down to a city in Samaria and *proclaimed the Christ there*' (Acts 8:4–5, my italics).

It is clear that there was a message – a 'word' – and that this word was centred on the news event of Jesus Christ.

The distinguished British New Testament scholar, C. H. Dodd, in his book, *The Apostolic Preaching and its development* (1935), pinpointed some basic elements which could be discerned in the preaching of the first Christians. He gave this collection of themes the label of 'the kerygma' (from the Greek word for proclamation).

These basic elements of the kerygma are as follows:

1. The promises of God in Old Testament times have been fulfilled. The Messiah (the Christ) has come.
2. The Christ is Jesus of Nazareth who:
   – Did good things wherever he went and worked miracles by the power of God.
   – Was crucified according to the purposes of God.
   – Was raised by God from the dead.
   – Is now exalted by God and given the title, 'Lord'.
   – Will come again for judgment and the restoration of all things.
3. Because of this, all who hear this message must repent and be baptised.

In 1983 I interviewed Billy Graham for a Mission England promotional video. One of the questions I asked was: 'What would you say is at the heart of the Gospel?'

He replied, 'The Gospel, for me, is the kerygma . . .'

We have heard much discussion and seen much evidence in the past twenty years of the 'charismatic movement'. The term is based on the Greek word *charis* meaning 'grace' and is to do with the grace-gifts which God gives to all believers. These gifts are described in the New Testament and are given to equip the churches to serve their Lord on earth. They mostly relate to particular ministries whether they be ministries of 'helps' or ministries of healing. The charismatic movement has gained a certain notoriety with some because it has refocused attention on such remarkable spiritual gifts as speaking in tongues, prophecy and words of knowledge. Perhaps the most controversial aspect of the charismatic movement is that many (but not all) of its spokesmen use the rare new Testament phrase 'baptised with the Holy Spirit' as a technical term for a necessary experience which all Christians need to have.

I believe that God has used the charismatic movement to bring a genuine renewal to many churches and thousands of individual Christians. Although I remain uneasy about some of the elements in charismatic teaching and, although I strongly oppose the idea of a necessary second blessing after conversion and identifying this as the 'baptism in the Spirit', I have to say I am grateful to God for what I have myself learned (and 'caught').

In particular the charismatic emphasis has brought home to many of us that God is alive and active now. The whole theme of spiritual warfare has been accentuated by the charismatic movement. Many of those who trusted most, gave most, and prayed most during Mission England were Charismatic believers who saw that a battle was joined and that sacrifice was called for.

So I thank God for the charismatic movement or renewal, but I believe the time has come for it to be balanced by a *kerygmatic movement and renewal*.

In an earlier chapter I have described how the churches are easily drawn into accommodating themselves to the secularised assumptions of much in contemporary society, or entrenching themselves so that they pretend the outside world isn't there. Both approaches tend to endanger the central place of the kerygma.

For the accommodationist Old Testament promises and talk about Jewish Messiahs are hardly relevant and meaningful. A Christ who worked miracles, whose death had a divine purpose and who was raised from his grave is either an embarrassment or is the end-product of misreporting by credulous enthusiasts. Talk of a judgment to come on which our eternal destiny depends is crude, threatening stuff which destroys any concept of a God of love.

There is no kerygma for the accommodationist. Only opinions which have a place in them for a benign father-figure of whom Jesus spoke and who, apart from all the contrary evidences of a suffering creation, wishes us well.

But as I look at those of us who are more in danger of cocooning ourselves from the uncomfortable realities of the world, I begin to suspect that the kerygma has also suffered some damage at our hands. We would not, of course, doubt any element in the package. The Old Testament is to us (at least in theory) as much a part of authoritative Scripture as the New. We believe Jesus worked miracles, died for our sins and rose again. We may be tempted to wish we were universalists, but judgment, heaven and hell are still boxes into which we place a tick.

In practice, however, the kerygma has been moved away from the centre of our attention and therefore of our habitual way of talking. As I look around the evangelical-charismatic spectrum (because there is a slightly uneasy but obvious 'alliance' between the two traditions), I can see several groups which have eased the kerygmatic emphases to the edges of their concerns and even of their message. There are, for example, evangelicals who are centring on such themes as justice and peacemaking – whether it be in the inner city or with regard to the arms race. There are others whose central concern is the authority of Scripture and the need to combat liberal influences. Alas, even such a worthy aim can lead to a set of priorities that leave little time for proclaiming the very message that is being defended.

There are those who see the battlefield to be within their own denominations and to do with resisting sacramentalism or pressing for greater doctrinal purity. Again there are others who see their agenda to be a breaking-free from the existing denominations which they see to be corrupted. Their task is to set up new fellowships with purified doctrine and proper patterns of leadership.

On top of all this there is the perpetual quest to find deeper teaching and fuller experience. The evangelical-charismatic alliance is not free of its conventions and teachers *where the agenda focuses on the needs of believers rather than the plight of the lost*. For such an agenda the kerygma is rarely deemed to be enough – there has to be more.

All these agendas exert tremendous diversionary pulls. They pull us away from having to encounter the unconverted and therefore having to share the kerygma. When one spends less and less time being put on one's mettle, the themes of the incarnation, Cross, Resurrection and judgment begin to drift to the edge of one's concerns. It is not that you cease to believe in the truth of the kerygma; it is that you cease to realise that these themes are central to the mission of God's people.

On three occasions in the year leading up to the writing of these words I have been involved in working parties trying to define priorities for evangelical Christians. In every case I have felt the need to plead for the specific mention of evangelism as a priority. This was not because the groups were opposed to evangelism. They assumed that evangelism and the evangel could be so taken for granted that it did not need to be mentioned. My constant fear is that it is very easy so to take something for granted that it gets ignored. I suspect that this is the case with many in the evangelical-charismatic alliance.

The kerygma will only be seen as central and relevant to those who are constantly confronting disbelief and trying to give a reason for the hope that they have. Where that confrontation becomes increasingly rare other themes – legitimate in themselves – can tend to usurp centre stage.

In the past decade or so a particular biblical theme has

been given centre stage in the proclamation of many evangelicals and charismatics. It is the theme of *the kingdom* and it has impeccable claims to be taken seriously. The idea of a different type of king establishing a different kind of kingdom (literally: reign) is in the Old Testament (e.g. Zech. 9). All scholars agree that 'the kingdom of God' was the central theme of Jesus's teaching and his strange donkey-back ride into Jerusalem on the first Palm Sunday was a deliberate staging of the scene foretold by Zechariah.

Jesus is described as preaching the good news of the kingdom (Matt. 4:23, 9:35). Is there therefore something at the heart of the actual teaching of the Lord that needs to be added to the kerygma? Was the proclamation of the Apostles slightly or seriously out of kilter in this regard? There can be no denying that they rarely talked about 'the kingdom of God' in their preaching.

More to the point – are present-day evangelicals and charismatics reading into the theme of the kingdom something that those first preachers knew wasn't there in the first place?

My own conviction is that Christ used kingdom language in a deliberately elusive way. As with the parables, people needed 'ears to hear' what he was really saying. The main point that was there to be 'heard' was that *he personally was the King*. Our modern western minds, however, look for precise definitions and agendas, and I fear that we inevitably put too developed an interpretation to Christ's words.

One thing is clear – evangelicals and charismatics are using kingdom language in at least two quite differing ways. There are those who have a very this-world concern and try to relate the challenge of God's righteousness to the society in which we live. The most eloquent spokesman for such a view is probably the American Jim Wallis, founder of the Sojourners Community, based in down-town Washington. In his book, *The New Radical*, he describes how after a time of rejection and involvement in the protest movement of the 60s, he 'wanted to take one last look at Christian faith'. His search took him to the Gospels and in particular to the Sermon on the Mount.

> The Sermon revealed to me what Jesus meant by the kingdom of God. In it, Jesus calls those who would follow him to a life that completely undermines the values and structures of this world and opens up possibilities of a new one. The way of life described in the Sermon is truly revolutionary, much deeper and more radical than the revolutionary movements of which I had had a taste. The way of Jesus overturns the assumptions of Right, Left and Middle, and presents a genuinely new option for both our personal and political lives. It calls for a life lived for God, for neighbor, for the poor, and even for enemies.
> I read on through the gospel narratives and the parables in which Jesus describes the ways that God's new order might become real in the lives of men and women during the political turmoil of first-century, Roman-occupied Palestine. The gospel story captured my imagination. All of my excitement about the new life I was discovering culminated for me when I read Matthew 25.[1]

The Matthew 25 passage with its account of the final judgment and the condemnation of those who did not feed the hungry, welcome the stranger and visit the sick and the prisoner, he describes as his 'conversion passage'.[2]

> I finally knew I wanted to be a follower of Jesus. Contrary to the message I had received from the church, Jesus's message was as political as it was personal, as economic as

---

[1] Lion (1983), p. 70.
[2] Ibid., p. 71.

it was spiritual, having as much to do with public life as individual devotion.[1]

In another book – *The Call to Conversion* – Wallis challenges Christians to reject their superficial, private-world conversions and to allow Christ to call them to a total conversion of their world-view as well as their morals. With such a conversion they could themselves be converting agents in a dark world of poverty, injustice, hatred and fear.

> Jesus is God made poor. His coming was prophesied to bring social revolution, and his kingdom would turn things upside down: the mighty would be brought low, the rich sent away empty, the poor exalted, the hungry satisfied (Luke 1: 52–3). Jesus identified himself with the weak, the outcast, the downtrodden. His kingdom undermines all economic systems that reward the rich and punish the poor.[2]

As Wallis is the first to admit, this message is poles apart from traditional Sunday School teaching. In the suburban heartlands of British and American evangelicalism it is a shocking and embarrassing message. It is the stuff that causes Conservative politicians to make garden-party speeches about 'left-wing trendy clergy' and much else. But such complaints are not good enough. One question has to be asked.

Is what Wallis is saying *true*? Was the heart of Christ's message a political one to do with overturning and setting up earthly kingdoms? If it was, why wasn't the kerygma of the first Christians stronger on such matters?

I would want to suggest that the apparent difference of

---

[1] Ibid., p. 72.
[2] Lion (1982), p. 59.

emphasis stems from the fact that the kerygma themes in the Acts of the Apostles show us the confrontational message of the primitive Church as it proclaimed Christ to the world. Their message was first and foremost that of a God who had broken into time and space in Jesus. Jesus had revealed his credentials through signs and wonders. When wicked men had rejected and crucified him, God had raised him up. He could not be avoided or destroyed. He was Lord and Christ. Those listening needed to change the way they looked at life and become his followers. That way lay salvation and being on the receiving end of 'times of refreshing' (Acts 3:19).

Those great kerygmatic sermons in the Acts of the Apostles do not tell the whole story – no evangelistic sermon can. They do not spell out what the Lordship of Christ would mean for those followers. We know as we look back over the centuries that conversion for the first Christians did in fact lead them to a situation where they were branded as public enemies of the Roman Empire. They were men and women who had to say 'We must obey God rather than men' (Acts 5:29), and there were times when that was threatening to the authorities as well as costly to the Christians.

It was not that the first Christians were political revolutionaries in their intention. The problem was that their primary allegiance was to a king other than Caesar, who had the highest of standards of righteousness. They were uncomfortable people to have around. They submitted only to the reign of Jesus.

When Paul was in the custody of Felix the Roman Governor in Caesarea, he was sent for to discuss 'faith in Christ Jesus' (Acts 24:24). The subject-matter of the discussion is revealing. 'As Paul discoursed on righteousness, self-control and the judgment to come, Felix was afraid . . .' Quite clearly Paul was an uncomfortable person to have around, even as a prisoner!

I do not believe that our confrontational message to the

world of our day should centre on social injustices. It should centre on the absolute justice and righteousness of the God we see in Christ, who loves us, who died for our sins, who was raised, who can come into our lives by his Spirit and *who calls us to follow him*. It is in the following of that righteous Christ today that we ought to be disturbing people. There is no such thing as a Christian country. We are not ruled by governments whose central policy-plank is to obey God. Christians are called to pray for and honour their rulers – but we have only one king and it is bound to lead to tensions.

In the first-century Roman Empire the only option was martyrdom. In modern democratic societies with established channels for pressure groups, legitimate protest and representatives in Parliament we have more options and we are meant to use them as means of demonstrating our love for our neighbour and our allegiance to the king.

I think men like Jim Wallis have much to teach us. I think evangelism is too often associated with a type of Christianity that sides with the powers of the time and claims that politics and the Gospel must never be confused. The message about (and the following of) a righteous Jesus cannot avoid being disturbing to the powers that be. I believe the evangelist who talks of the grace of God as seen in the coming, death and resurrection of Christ is given extra credentials when he or she is seen to be speaking for a group who set themselves the highest standards and are renowned for compassion and identification with the sinned-against sections of society.

Having said this, I do not believe we should present a socialised interpretation of the kingdom as if it were the sum total of the meaning of that term. While it is true that the Gospel is this-worldly as well as next-worldly and while God is concerned about the material as well as the spiritual, there still remains a danger that hearers will misinterpret kingdom language handled in this way. Social issues are often tied tightly into secular political policies. People often think emotionally rather than rationally about such matters. When preachers tread such waters, people all too easily misinterpret them and put them into 'right wing' or 'left wing' pigeon-holes.

At the end of the day we must remember that Jesus said that his kingdom is 'not of this world'.

There is, however, a totally different way in which some evangelicals (and especially charismatics) have been using kingdom language. Another American, John Wimber, has become a focal figure for this other kingdom emphasis.

> The church is also the instrument of the kingdom. The disciples not only proclaimed the kingdom, they demonstrated the words and miracles of the kingdom. Jesus told Peter that 'the gates of Hades will not overcome it [the church]' (Matt. 16:18). The 'gates of Hades' are the strongholds of evil and death, satanic powers that seek to destroy us (Eph. 6:10–12). As Christ's instruments, we war on these strongholds, replacing their dominion with the kingdom of God.[1]

Wimber, a warm bulky genial man with a remarkable ministry, is only one of many who see the kingdom emphasis in the Gospel not as a call to be politically disturbing, but as a call to be spiritually powerful. The kerygma included reference to the signs and wonders of Jesus. If Jesus lives in us by his Holy Spirit, surely we should expect to see those same signs and wonders in our ministry – not least in our evangelism?

And that word 'expect' is crucial. In *Power Evangelism – signs and wonders today*, Wimber argues powerfully that much contemporary Christianity (not least evangelicalism) is affected by the prevailing secular world view of the times.

---

[1] *Power Evangelism* (Hodder & Stoughton), p. 21.

'Our expectations are affected by our world view,' he writes.[1] 'If Christians have a world view that is affected by Western materialism, they will probably deny that signs and wonders are for today.'[2]

Wimber is unanswerable when he points out that in both Jesus and the Apostles we see a clash of the kingdom of light against the kingdom of darkness. Jesus and the Apostles were more than preachers. They had ministries which challenged and defeated Satan's effects on people. The blind were given sight, the lame helped to walk, lepers cured, demons were cast out, even the dead were – on occasion – raised.

One has to admit that the sort of things that are described in the Gospels and Acts have little in common with the Christianity of an orderly, middle-class congregation sitting, Bibles open, listening to a classic exposition, before going out to be barely distinguishable from anyone else. 'The disciples expelled demons,' writes Wimber. 'We also advance the Kingdom of God in the same way: overthrowing every contrary spirit in the name of our King.'[3]

Do we?

Wimber not only points to the discrepancy between New Testament Christianity and the brand that is typical today, which has no dynamic expectations of God's power. He also points to the experience of the younger churches in the Third World.

> Power evangelism is flourishing in non-technological countries. People living in these countries are often animists – that is, they believe there are actual spirits that hold people in bondage and the supernatural power of the Holy Spirit is needed to break their hold. A colleague of mine from Fuller Theological Seminary, Dr Charles

[1] Ibid., p. 93.
[2] Ibid., p. 95.
[3] Ibid., p. 100.

Kraft, tells about going to Nigeria and attempting to teach the Book of Romans to a small tribe. After a few months, they came to him, very politely, and said that they appreciated his teaching, but it was not relevant to their needs. What they needed was wisdom for dealing with spirits that plagued the villagers every night, something that Kraft readily admitted he was not trained to do.[1]

The main thrust of Wimber's argument is that 'power evangelism' is for all of us if we would only believe in God's power and act accordingly. He spells out (with remarkable anecdotes) how he and others known to him have had 'words of knowledge' about total strangers which have led to the conversion of such people. He describes casting out demons, and healings that led to the conversion of an entire family.

He contrasts this 'power evangelism' with what he describes as 'programmatic evangelism' where people are trained to present the Gospel in structured ways that assume the problem in the unbeliever is always intellectual. Power evangelism clearly touches the parts that programmatic evangelism never reaches!

I think that Wimber is unfair to so-called programme evangelism. Most structured ways of presenting the Gospel are essentially kerygmatic. They are ways of putting the context of the Gospel message across to those who want to know what we believe and why. To say that they are primarily to do with the intellect rather than the Spirit is to underestimate the inherent power of God's Word. A structured presentation of the Gospel can often be a 'power encounter'. But he is also correct to suggest that we often engage in a technique-dominated evangelism that leaves no place for the Holy Spirit to break in.

It would be a mistake to play off the charismatic against

[1] Ibid., p. 52.

the kerygmatic. Word and Spirit must go together. The very people Wimber points to in the Acts of the Apostles – such as Philip who did ' great signs and miracles' (Acts 8:13) – were also the people who 'preached the Word wherever they went'.

Wimber's real challenge, however, is not that we should change our message. It is that we should change our manner. We have got to de-secularise our expectations and to be open to the power of God's Spirit to break through just as he did in Apostolic times.

Wimber rejects the dispensational view that the New Testament period was a special one before the canon of Scripture was formed and that now we have the Bible, signs and wonders are withdrawn. 'Power encounters' where God is seen to overthrow the power of Satan should be expected today and they can happen today.[1]

I find it hard to disagree with the main thrust of his teaching. What I fear, however, is that the teaching of Wimber and others like him can lead to false expectations. For all the power evangelism of the New Testament era, the Middle East was not swept lock, stock and barrel into the kingdom. For all the anecdotes that Wimber can tell (and I do not doubt them), California remains a pretty secular state. Power evangelism is not the magic ingredient that will

---

[1] There are many who suggest that the Western world is moving away from a rational to a post-rational culture through the influence of such factors as television and rock music. In parallel with this development there is an increase in reported instances of overt demonic activity. Could it be that the devil alters his tactics according to the way people think and have their attitudes changed? Reports from those working with more primitive cultures in other parts of the world would suggest this. Could it be that John Wimber and others who call us to a power ministry are pointing us to the weapons that are needed for the warfare of the 1980s and 1990s post-rational age? Those of us, like myself, who have reservations ought to ask whether we are wanting to cling on to the more familiar weapons of yesterday's battles in a more rational era.

suddenly sweep the people of our nation back into the churches. There is no one thing that will.

I do not believe that a signs-and-wonders ministry is for all, or that it is meant to be exercised in large gatherings (such as football-stadium meetings). I have attended meeting where the preacher (*not* John Wimber) has claimed to be pursuing the power-evangelism approach and felt deeply disturbed at what I saw. I think there is a real danger of witting or unwitting emotional exploitation taking place in these sorts of meeting. I do not think the general public would be attracted to such activities and I would rate the true evangelistic potential of this sort of gathering as limited.

Evangelists with a public-healing ministry are nothing new and one has to admit that their record over the years has been somewhat chequered. The New Testament healings were nearly always carried out away from the limelight, and the healing ministry commended in those pages seems to me to put more emphasis on corporate, prayerful activity rather than dramatic solo turns by individuals with a particular gift. My fear is that immature Christians will be beguiled by the thought of having power and try to do set-piece power evangelism from platforms rather than in the unstructured ups and downs of everyday life which is where we see power evangelism happening in the New Testament.

We need to remember also that the New Testament not only affirms signs and wonders, it also warns against unhealthy dependence upon them. Jesus criticised those who needed signs and wonders before they would believe (Matt. 12:39). He also forecast that 'false Christs and false prophets' would appear and 'perform great signs and miracles to deceive even the elect...' (Matt. 24:24). Not everything that appears to be miraculous is of God.

We must not be blind to the carnal attraction of the signs-and-wonders agenda. We live in a power-hungry age and rank and file people are usually deeply conscious of their lack of power to change anything. A shallow message that promises power to those who respond could be a magnet to the unbalanced and also to the modern-day equivalent of Simon the Sorcerer (Acts 8).

My point here is not to suggest that we should ignore John Wimber's contribution. That would be foolish. Rather I want to show the dangers of seeing his teaching and his particular practices as a bandwagon to be jumped on in the hope that it will take us all to our evangelistic destination quickly and without difficulties.

A strong emphasis on the primacy of the *Word* (which God may choose to confirm with signs and wonders) is surely the safeguard. But those of us who want to be alert to the dangers must not make that the excuse for the sort of disbelief which thwarts the Lord's ability to do great works.

Any message highlighting God's ability to do signs and wonders as much today as in the Apostles' time, however, needs to be balanced with other aspects of New Testament Christianity. We need to hear Paul talking about 'the whole Creation groaning as in pains of childbirth' and being in 'bondage to decay' (Rom. 8:21–2). We need to realise that as creatures even 'we ourselves, who have the firstfruits of the Spirit, groan inwardly as we wait eagerly for our adoption as sons, the redemption of our bodies' (v. 23). We need to remember that Paul could talk about being 'hard pressed', 'perplexed', 'persecuted' and 'struck down'. (2 Cor. 4:8, 9).

There are no easy victories in spiritual warfare and sometimes our lot will be that of being able to do no more than 'stand' (Eph. 6:13). Sometimes I get the impression that, because of God's power, I should expect to ride roughshod over all problems and never be sick. In fairness, people like John Wimber do not say such ridiculous things, but there is often a discrepancy between what is said and what is 'heard'.

Properly spelled out there are three tenses to a healthy

Christianity. There is the past. It is rooted in history. We have a story to tell from a previous age about God coming in Christ. The Cross of Christ and his amazing Resurrection are at the heart of that story and we have a duty to keep on telling 'the old, old story of Jesus and his love'.

But our message is a message of hope. Christianity has a future tense. Because of the Cross we have the prospect of heaven and a judgment which holds no terrors for the one who will judge us is the one who died for our sins and offers forgiveness. We can look forward with firm hopes to a world where 'the dwelling of God is with men . . . They will be his people, and God himself will be with them . . . He will wipe every tear from their eyes. There will be no more death or mourning or crying or pain, for the old order of things has passed away' (Rev. 21:3–4). The best, as the saying goes, is yet to be.

What the charismatic understanding of the kingdom does is to remind us that Christianity has a present tense. The Christ who worked in wonderful ways in the past reserves the right to do so now. Jesus is alive and we are his followers and soldiers fighting his battles at his side. 'For our struggle is not against flesh and blood, but against the rulers, against the authorities, against the powers of this dark world and against the spiritual forces of evil in the heavenly realms' (Eph. 6:12).

But people get hurt in battles. Christ did not spare himself the Cross and he does not protect us from carrying our own crosses either. When 'power evangelism' thinking is shorn of a shallow triumphalism and contains a place for suffering and waiting patiently for better things to come, then it is truly New Testament Christianity.

And nothing else will do.

12

Can we reach Whole Communities?

Some years ago a series of small advertisements appeared in the Christian press. The slogan they carried was something like this: 'Evangelise the world through car stickers.'

If only it was that simple.

Luis Palau came to London in 1983 and 1984 for an exhausting schedule of evangelistic meetings. Alongside the umbrella title of *Mission to London* there was this theme: 'Let the whole of London hear the voice of God!'

The question I want to ask is simple. Can the whole of anywhere hear anything? Can the world be 'reached'? Can a nation be 'reached'? Can we 'reach' whole communities for Christ?

To some extent it all depends on what we mean by 'reached'. Again, the question calls for a more careful examination of what we mean by 'communities'. Evangelical folklore encourages us to believe that the Wesleys and Whitfield 'reached' the United Kingdom of their day. The evangelical awakening changed the course of the nation's history. So we are told, and it may well be that there is some substance to the claim.

What we must not glibly say is that if it happened then it can also happen now. Today's world is very different and one of the main differences is in the way communities organise themselves and communicate within themselves. The contemporary,

Can we reach Whole Communities?

industrialised electronic community has no parallel in history. The walk of life in the second half of the twentieth century takes us along untrodden paths.

In the fourth chapter of John's Gospel we read of Christ's encounter with the woman at the well in Sychar, Samaria. She was so affected by her discussion with Jesus that she ran into the town, shouting, 'Come, see a man who told me everything I ever did. Could this be the Christ?' The next words we read are: 'They came out of the town and made their way towards him' (John 4:29–30). We later read, 'Many of the Samaritans from that town believed in him because of the woman's testimony' (v. 39). Later still we read 'many more became believers' (v. 41).

Quite clearly the community was significantly if not largely 'reached' for Christ. A large number of people were made aware of the person of Christ and heard his teaching. Out of this large number a significant proportion came to a belief 'that this man really is the Saviour of the world' (v. 42).

I want to suggest that this sort of impact upon a community requires not only mass awareness of the centre of proclamation (in this case, Jesus himself), but also extremely effective internal communication networks so that the same messages or signals are being sent from person to person and group to group in all directions within a short space of time.

Curiously enough this is far more likely to happen in a slow-moving, non-industrial community than in the sorts of communities created within modern, developed societies.

In the little town of Sychar the pace of life was slow. Work, food and water-gathering, buying and selling were all communal activities calling for conversation and making possible the exchange of news and views. Differing generations lived close to each other and needed each other. Work was near one's place of residence and recreation – such as it was – took a communal rather than private dimension. Above all, gossip was the spice of life.

In other words – news travelled and usually travelled fast.

The situation in today's European or North American city and suburb is very different. The pace of life is fast – thanks to motor-cars (usually containing lone occupants). Work is often miles away from the place where one sleeps – hence the term 'dormitory suburb'. Food-gathering does not have to be a communal activity and rarely is. You don't walk to the well and chat with your friends as the water-containers are winched up. It is piped into the house. (I've heard of an Indian village that abandoned a piped-water scheme because it destroyed community life.)

Recreation is either privatised via television or calls for the creation of self-contained, single-agenda mini-communities. Sometimes these are also well away from one's residence.

In this modern community, communication is tightly channelled through radio, TV and the press. One may know one's immediate neighbours and the members of one's club or church, but the gossip stops there. Conversation tends to be functional rather than relational.

In other words, news doesn't travel – it has to be sent via media which are controlled by people with editorial concerns, who decide what is and what is not worth broadcasting.

It is hardly surprising that in spite of great population density in many contemporary communities, there is an epidemic of loneliness. It is even worth questioning whether – outside of villages – communities still exist. Is London a community? Is Birmingham or Liverpool or Newcastle? Are such places not better described as population concentrations?

Because mass media are responsible for controlling so much of our communication and because most of our communities are residential rather than relational, many

Can we reach Whole Communities?

people have little awareness of what is being said two blocks away. If a woman came running into Sheffield city centre saying, 'Come and see a man', she would probably be run over in the first few minutes. She would certainly be ignored by the vast majority who were out and about, because in most cases such people are on the move for functional reasons (to catch buses or to go shopping) rather than looking for gossip opportunities.

In modern residential rather than relational communities, churches are in no man's land. Their affairs do not warrant attention from the mass media on the one hand, nor are they so small and localised that they fit into the mini-communities comprising people in their immediate neighbourhoods and families. In a sense churches can even be destructive of a community. They are rivals to each other and form single-agenda, time-consuming communities within the community. They form gossip traps containing the flow of messages rather than releasing or enhancing such interpersonal communication. (In fairness, the same inhibitions are also caused by sports clubs and hobbies groups – all tend to be cherished as boltholes from a confusing and impersonal world.).

A closer examination of a modern population concentration reveals, I suggest, that the average person is aware of three different dimensions to community.

First, he is aware of the *mini-community* of his own family, immediate neighbours and circle of colleagues at work.

Second, he is aware of the *mega-community*. This is the world brought into his consciousness by the mass media – TV, radio and newspaper. He feels he knows presidents, prime ministers, pop stars, sports personalities, TV announcers and disc jockeys.

He is usually more aware of the people in this electronic mega-community (or 'global village' as Marshall McLuhan called it) than he is of what is going on in the few square miles around his place of residence.

This then brings us to the third dimension of community – *the medium community*. It consists of the actual, geographical suburb or town. The map identifies it as a community. There are civic arrangements. Rates may be levied and candidates may represent such places in national parliaments, but they are often the least real communities of all.

With this in mind let me ask the question once again. How *do* we reach contemporary communities with the Gospel? To put it another way – how do we get awareness of and presentation of the Gospel outside the ecclesiastical cliques we call churches?

It seems to me that we have to recognise that our churches are all elements of the medium community. We are too big and generalised to be in the mini-communities and we are too small to impress the editors who decide what is sufficiently big or interesting to be part of the content of the mega-community. We have to take calculated steps, therefore, to remedy these weaknesses.

The answer, I suggest, is that we have to operate within the communities of which people have most awareness – the mega and the mini. If something becomes news in the mega community then everyone is aware of it. That does not mean that many are likely to have their convictions changed, however. Information through radio, TV, the press and advertising may excite interest and curiosity. It may even tempt people to sample. It rarely, however, *converts*.

When the woman rushed into first-century Sychar, her shouts did not convert. What they did achieve was to arouse interest. Without that arousal of interest there would have been no subsequent conversions. In today's electronic, post-industrial society the woman's shouts are like those shouts in dreams I mentioned earlier. They become swallowed up into the apathy that mass communities generate towards that which either does not affect one's personal affairs or is not important enough to make the headlines.

Can we reach Whole Communities?

In the UK (and, I sense, in many other developed countries) God does not fall into the 'as seen on TV' bracket – at least, not significantly. Clive Calver put his finger on it early in the Mission England planning. 'There is not enough "God-awareness" in the UK,' he said. 'We have to plan something that will create that awareness.' Clive knew that getting 'God-awareness' firmly planted in the mega-community would not convert anybody – but it was essential to have that awareness to build on if we were to mount any large-scale evangelistic project.

Some time ago I was invited to meet a group of ministers in a Scottish city and to talk about the possibility of a large-scale mission in their area. Again and again I met friendly but firm resistance from the ministers. They were convinced that 'large- scale' missions inhibited local-church evangelism. I argued that, properly planned, large-scale projects had quite the opposite effect. I asked if they could produce a shred of evidence or serious research that could back their contention. The truth was that they could not.

What they were doing was abandoning the mega-community. They were not alone. It has been fashionable for some twenty years or so to say that the only true evangelism is that which comes from the local church. It sounds so correct – so 'biblical'. The effect of twenty years of doing this, however, is that the general public who are outside our congregations and their fringe contacts have less and less awareness of God. Without that awareness the search for Christ cannot be started.

Does this mean that I am wanting to downgrade local-church evangelism? Far from it. As I hope to show, the local church is still our ace card in evangelism, but we must get our understanding of communities corrected.

So we need to get the Gospel into the mega world more effectively than at present – and this means something more than an increase of religious television or radio programmes.

They suffer from being type-cast and audiences self-select whether they want to watch or not. Branded Christian television programmes tend to be watched by branded Christians. God has got to become *news*.

News in the mega dimension, however, will not convert people. The Gospel has got to be presented more effectively in the mini-communities. And here we are indeed being 'biblical'. Church-growth researchers, such as Dr Win Arn, have suggested that the astonishing growth of the primitive church was because the evangelism of that period tapped into the natural links of families, servants and friends. It was *household* evangelism.

The Philippian jailor was baptised – 'he and all his family' (Greek – 'household') (Acts 16:33). Cornelius the centurion was led to call for Peter and ask for an exposition of the Gospel. When Peter and his friends arrived he found that 'Cornelius was expecting them and had called together his relatives and close friends' (Acts 10:24).

This corresponds closely to the findings of my simple survey mentioned earlier in Chapter 8. After the influence of the local church it was clear that family and friends are the most effective ways by which the Gospel is shared and people are converted.

We have got so to organise our church life and recognise this factor that we enhance household evangelism today. Every person is caught up in a network of relationships – family, friends, neighbours and colleagues. If people enjoy being Christians and have some ability to explain what it is they have discovered in Christ, then there is far more chance that this most natural sort of evangelism will take place.

One friend of mine was converted in her mid 30s. She was so excited by the discovery (it came after a heartbreaking divorce) that she gossiped enthusiastically around her 'household'. Within two years her mother and her two sisters

Can we reach Whole Communities?

and their husbands had come to the same liberating experience.

The vision for this and the motivation can only come from our local churches set in the medium-community. More than that, I want to say that the medium-community church is the key to penetrating both the mini and the mega worlds. Through our worship, teaching, training and vision-setting, we can send our members back into their networks of relationships better able to witness and explain the Gospel. But there is something more. When local churches stop living as isolated congregations and link up with others, their united resources can create projects big enough to break into the mega-community. There comes a time when the editors have to admit that we are news.

This is what we were able to do in *Mission England*. With 6,000 churches co-operating we were able to mount a project that made headlines. I remember in the early days of the project being phoned by a reporter of the *Daily Telegraph*. I told him of our plans for training and motivating large numbers of Christians. I told him about the proposed visit of Billy Graham and the holding of evangelistic meetings in six cities.

'And where will he be preaching?' he asked. 'Town halls, I suppose?'

'No,' I replied. 'We plan to put him in football stadiums.'

There was a stunned silence and then with a voice that showed much more respect and interest, he said: 'This really is *big*'

It was – but we were only able to do it because a huge number of churches across the country pooled their resources. They were the key factor.

The Mission England strategy was based upon this conviction of the mini- and mega-communities being more 'real' to most people than their geographical medium-communities.

Through the co-operating churches we got through to individual Christians. We tried to 'sell' them the vision for praying in triplets for their immediate friends, neighbours and colleagues. This focused people on evangelism within the mini-community.

We encouraged people 'to break new ground' in their personal relationships and witnessing. We offered a course on 'Christian conversation'. As the great stadium meetings drew near we pushed hard on the 'Operation Andrew' scheme, stressing yet again the need to get alongside friends and neighbours and to bring them to hear the evangelist.

It was this side of things – this penetration into hundreds of thousands of 'households' or mini-communities – that was the basis upon which the so-called mass evangelism of Billy Graham took place. The general public became aware of the proposed Billy Graham meetings through the large-scale advertising, the million-plus door-to-door visitation and the news items in press and on radio and TV. But we knew that if people were to fill those stadiums they would be got there through personal relationships with Christians. That is why the phrase 'not mass evangelism but personal evangelism on a massive scale' has so much substance to it. From the medium-communities we penetrated the mini-communities by the hundreds of thousands and this in turn made possible the operation within the mega-community.

But the prospect of the mega-event was what motivated so much of the mini-activity! This is why one can do an effective city-wide or region-wide project more easily than something that centres on the medium-community. When one is operating at that level the mass media are not interested. The medium-community media (local radio and newspaper) rarely, in fact, deeply influence their constituencies. It is hard to create general awareness of any project working solely in this dimension.

Can we reach Whole Communities?

That does not mean we should give up. In 1986 I was invited to lead a mission in Woodley, a dormitory suburb of Reading. All the local churches (two Anglican, a Methodist/URC united church, a Baptist, an Independent Charismatic Fellowship and the Roman Catholic congregation) were involved in the mission.

While we attracted some small interest in the local newspapers and radio station there was little aid to our cause. Our strategy was to concentrate, yet again, on the mini-communities. We started prayer triplets and emphasised personal friendship and witnessing. Our mission lasted two weeks. In the first week we held sixty-four small, usually house-based, gatherings where people were invited for a meal and a discussion about the claims of Christianity. We trained some fifty or so members of the local churches to lead those meetings.

The key was to find people who literally gathered their 'households' together – family, friends, neighbours and colleagues.

Some 700 people, many with very tenuous links to the churches, attended. Quite apart from the fact that these meetings caused many to begin thinking seriously about the Gospel, they were worth doing because some fifty or so Christians were made to state and explain their faith in front of others. The excitement and joy of this were remarkable.

That natural, dialogue-evangelism forced the Christians to depend on God's help in a way that blessed them deeply. It also became a key stepping-stone for many in their journey towards faith.

In the second week of the mission we focused attention on public meetings in a centrally-placed marquee. Overall, some 6 per cent of all who attended came forward for counselling. While this was a respectable figure, the overall attendance was disappointing – an average of about 300 people per evening out of a total population of some 30,000.

It revealed once again the weakness of attempting to work in the medium-community.

On the other hand, a considerable number of those who 'came forward' were people who had attended a dialogue-supper evening the previous week. What success there was in the central meetings was based on prior work and existing relationships at 'household' or mini-community level.

(As in the case of Mission England our follow-up strategy was based on inviting enquirers to nurture groups. Yet again, therefore, we tried to cash in on the fact that as most people are more comfortable in the mini- and mega-community contexts so their first experience of Christian fellowship and teaching should be set in one of these dimensions.)

I confess to a certain amount of irritation with my own jargon in this chapter! However, it has been deliberate. We need to identify what we are doing and to be brutally realistic and accurate in our talk. Mission England did not 'reach' England and Mission Woodley did not reach Woodley. Both were honourable attempts. Both highlight lessons we must learn.

What are my conclusions?

First we need to have a realistic understanding of what we mean by 'reaching' a community. The only people known to me who have tried to bring some precision into such a discussion are those associated with the 'Missions Advanced Research and Communication Centre' in Monrovia, California.

They have developed, together with the Lausanne Committee for World Evangelism, a way of looking at the global evangelistic task in terms of reaching 'people groups'. Accordingly, they talk in terms of *reached* peoples and 'unreached' peoples. What do these terms mean?

First, a people group is defined as 'any significantly large sociological grouping of individuals who perceive themselves

Can we reach Whole Communities?

to have a common affinity for one another'.[1] By this token a people group could be an ethnic minority or it could be a social class, a language group or even a profession such as golfers on the American, European or Asian PGA circuits. Because they are close-knit groups, one can make most impact with the Gospel when one is either a member or is accepted within the people group.

The people-group strategy shows that there are fluid, non-geographical medium-communities that have many of the communication qualities I have been reserving for the mini-community or household. This is undoubtedly true and we need to take it into our thinking. I do not believe, however, that one can base an entire missionary strategy on a sort of progression through one people group after another. In modern developed countries there are large numbers of people who are devoid of any sense of belonging to any sort of group. After a while, the people-group way of analysing and planning becomes faintly ridiculous with huge lists of differing, identifiable groups all calling for their own missionary strategies.

But, second, the people-group thinkers have devised a definition for a *reached* community, and this is helpful to my purpose in this chapter. 'An unreached people,' writes Dayton, 'is a group that is less than 20 per cent practising Christian.'[2] This means that if a community has 20 per cent of its members who go to church (the only measurable way of judging the practice of Christianity) then it is 'reached'. Presumably, from the point of considering whether people need to be *sent* into these communities with the Gospel (which is what 'mission' means) there is little need. One can expect mission to be generated within the community from the 20 per cent who practise their faith.

---

[1] *That Everyone May Hear*, by Edward Dayton (MARC), p. 22.
[2] Ibid., p. 27.

While I find this useful, it does not help me in the matter of judging either human projects or spiritual awakenings. What I would find helpful is a form of judging whether a town or county over a five- (or at the most ten-) year period can be said to have been *reached*.

The MARC approach is a somewhat static way of measuring things. A community may have 20 per cent of its members practising Christianity, but the truth could be that the influence of the faith is declining fast. If ten years earlier the figure stood at 35 per cent, can one classify the people group as reached? I need a definition of reaching a community that enables me to set goals before and measure attainment afterwards.

The Gospel story of the woman in Sychar suggests that there are two aspects to a reached community. The first is a high level of public awareness of Gospel and of the location and identity of those who are proclaiming it. This public awareness must not depend on a widespread desire on the part of the population to seek that information. The information has to be projected into the community so that at least 75 per cent of the population is aware of what is going on.

After her discussion with Jesus by the well, 'the woman went back to the town and said to the people, "Come, see a man who told me everything I ever did. Could this be the Christ?" *They came out of the town and made their way towards him*' (John 4:28–9, my italics). Sychar was a small place and news travelled fast. The information was so effectively communicated that there was a huge response at the level of curiosity and awareness. It is surely not overstating the situation to suggest that 75 per cent of the population was 'reached' at this preliminary level of awareness.

I should like to suggest, therefore, that we take this as a yardstick. For an evangelistic project to 'reach' a town, city or region there must be 75 per cent public awareness of the project and the issues it stands for.

Can we reach Whole Communities?

At this level Mission England can be adjudged a success. As a result of good public relations, widespread advertising, wholesale visitation and massive penetration from the churches into the mini-communities, the Gallup polls taken in Bristol, Sunderland and Liverpool revealed public-awareness levels of 85 per cent upwards.

However, widespread awareness and temporary curiosity are not enough. The second aspect of a 'reached' community must take the shape of a significant percentage of people within that community becoming openly committed to Christ as a result of encountering the proclamation and the proclaimers. No figures or percentages are stated in the story of the woman of Sychar. I cannot believe, however, in the light of what it describes, that less than 20 per cent of those who went out to hear Jesus made a commitment. It would seem reasonable to me to assume far more than that. However, I suggest we agree with the MARC figures here and settle for 20 per cent, except to say that in project thinking we are talking about a 20 per cent increase on the figure that existed before the event or programme in question.

By this token Mission England failed. In none of the areas in question was 20 per cent of the population brought to commitment. But the figure of 20 per cent is not an unreasonable standard to set. It has almost certainly been reached in rural communities as a result of times of spiritual revival. It probably happened in the Hebridean revival in the years shortly after the Second World War. With this sort of mass movement there is every reason to expect a powerful momentum to be created.

Obviously, we cannot *plan* for such a response. We can, however, use such a standard to assess the degree of effectiveness of some large-scale mission or programme. My first conclusion, therefore, is that for planning and assessing community-wide evangelistic projects we consider that community to be reached if there is 75-per-cent public awareness of the project and its message and if this is followed by a 20-per-cent increase of the adult population with a commitment to Christ. In the case of this second aspect it might be both helpful and humbling to speak in terms of the percentage success towards the goal of a reached community. In Mission England the national percentage effectiveness is tiny. However, I can think of some villages and neighbourhoods that were at least 25 per cent reached.

There is a second conclusion I wish to draw from this discussion. Quite simply, there are no short-cuts. We cannot evangelise the world through car stickers, the Church of England, Billy Graham or any one agency or method.

In an earlier chapter I pointed out that religious radio and television are hardly likely to 'reach' communities. This is because they are, in the main, listened to and watched by those who so choose. They do not create that 75-per-cent awareness and most certainly would not give rise to a 20-per-cent gain in Christian commitment. In 1986 the BBC announced a 'dramatic increase in audiences for religious radio programmes'. Nearly two million extra listeners tuned in. I do not think that the excellence of the BBC was the reason. That growth in interest, I suggest, came from what was going on away from the radio-set. David Winter, Head of Religious Programmes, openly acknowledged this. 'My guess is,' he said, 'that these statistics back up the impression created by correspondence, telephone calls and week-by-week contact with listeners – that the tide of interest in religious belief and experience is *rising*, not falling.'[1] In other words, the mass media cash in on what is happening rather than create it. They can reinforce belief, but are less effective at creating it.

[1] Press release, July 1986.

Can we reach Whole Communities?

So is there a key? Can we reach communities? Yes, we can, or at least we can play our part so that we do not hinder the Holy Spirit.

What is clear to me is that we must start from the places where we are, and that we must see clearly a strategy for the next step.

Where we are is in our churches in those medium-communities. For all the problems this medium-community holds, we must affirm our local churches and make them the base as long as one thing is clear. Congregations must reject isolationism and see the need to pool resources with other congregations – not as an occasional practice but as part of a continuous strategy.

Where we need to go is also clear to me. The fundamental community and the one that is most 'real' to most people is the mini-community or household. Our churches must see their primary, evangelistic task as that of equipping their members to *be* Christian and to share Christ in their everyday relationships with family, neighbours, friends and colleagues. What has to be avoided energetically is churches allowing their members to find and foster their mini-communities within the wider church membership. The Christian, like his or her master, has to be incarnated in the world that does not yet acknowledge Christ as Lord. There can be no evangelism without this first building brick in place.

13

Who Cares?

The phone rang at breakfast time on April 1st. It was my vicar (I was in my first curacy).

'The baby's on the way,' he said.

Mary and I (plus our frenetic beagle) hurriedly flung our cornflakes and milk bottle into a carrier-bag and rushed to take over the vicar's household while his wife produced their second child.

Everyone in our East London congregation knew that the couple were hoping for a boy. The midwife arrived, the tension mounted and then came that awesome sound of a newborn cry. Mark had come into the world.

I come now to the point of my story. We put up no posters and we hired no public-relations experts. We had no loudspeaker vans driving round the parish. Yet within half an hour the presents and greetings cards began to arrive and they kept on coming.

When people are excited about something they have to talk about it and the message spreads . . .

This has been a book reflecting on the bewildering task of evangelising a nation. It began by posing the question of how one 'reaches' a modern, developed nation for Christ. We have considered many of the lessons learned from the largest and most fully co-ordinated evangelistic project in England's history – *Mission England*. I was privileged to be one of its

Who Cares?

originators and to head the entire exercise. It is now history.

But England has not been 'reached'. There were great gains. History may well show – as the Archbishop of Canterbury kindly said in an encouraging letter to me – that there will be 'a rich harvest' as a result of it. But history will not show that this one project in itself evangelised a nation.

To reach a nation is, humanly speaking, an impossible dream. But we must dream it none the less and ask God to empower us and keep us faithful in its pursuit.

I have worked away at trying to motivate evangelism for many years. One thing is clear to me from what I have seen. *Where people are excited about God they don't need to be told to evangelise. They just do it!* The problem we face with the vast majority of church members is that either they have never had a love relationship with God or they have lost their first love.

That is why I have never forgotten that April day in East London when my godson, Mark, was born into the world for what turned out to be a short but gentle, loving life. People were excited so they knocked on doors, picked up phones and called over the fence to their neighbours.

Oh that it might happen to celebrate the birth of God's son!

There is a story about St Paul that means much to me. It is told in the seventeenth chapter of the Acts of the Apostles. Paul had been the centre of too much hostile attention in the Greek town of Berea. Eventually the beleaguered Christians decided to pack him off, out of harm's way. He went to Athens and the plan was that he would wait there for Silas and Timothy to join him. But Paul did more than wait. He reflected on what he saw. 'While Paul was waiting for them in Athens, he was greatly distressed to see that the city was full of idols' (Acts 17:16).

Paul was a man deeply excited about God, but there was this second emotion. He was able to feel distressed for those who were spiritually lost. This second emotion is even rarer than the first in contemporary Christianity. We have relatively few church members who are excited about God and even fewer who feel distress for their unconverted fellow countrymen.

I have to say that as I sit through some of the debates in the General Synod and as I sit through the cheerful and emotional activities of many a praise rally I find a common strand. *There is far too little concern for the lost.*

The plain fact of the matter is that the question of reaching the nation for Christ is not on the agendas of any denomination or group of churches known to me. Nor is it obviously written deep in the hearts of any significant percentage of Christians.

We have been infected with the experiential, self-indulgent spirit of the age. If, while we do what we enjoy doing, we can bring others on board so much the better. If not, then as long as we are enjoying ourselves in God's name that is good enough.

But evangelism is *not* about Christians enjoying themselves. It is about Christians sharing that joy and sometimes having their smiles wiped off their faces. It is – and here we must listen to the Wimbers of this world – about spiritual warfare and fighting against the powers of darkness. Satan rules the affairs of too many people, but he will not give up his prizes without a fight. I think he likes to see Christians enjoying themselves!

Paul was distressed in Athens. Jesus wept as he contemplated the spiritual disaster facing his beloved Jerusalem. John Knox is reported to have prayed, 'Give me Scotland or I die!' Unless something of that divine dismay characterises our churches, evangelism will always be a shallow business.

How does one 'reach a nation'? First of all we need to blend both idealism and realism. We should long for full churches and many more of them. We should long for greater love, forgiveness and righteousness in the affairs of the nation. We should pray and work for a nation that is clear about good and evil and yet is compassionate for the many who fall into wrongdoing. We should dream of a nation that wants to declare war not on other nations but on poverty, sickness and ignorance whether it be within its boundaries or beyond.

If any approximation of these things is ever to happen I believe it will have to be founded on a spread of the Gospel of Jesus Christ.

That is the ideal – the dream. But it needs to be matched with a realism. There are no instant solutions when it comes to evangelism. No new method or theology will win the nation to Christ. We need to work away at the small things as well as the big. We need to stand by the small inner-city and rural churches where they may never win prizes for numerical growth. We need to thank God for the joy of small things.

I have never forgotten a simple phrase used by Tom Philips of the Billy Graham team at a training conference I attended. 'Evangelism is *work*!'

He was right, and I have to admit that many of us who are good at dreaming dreams are often more than a little work-shy. To plan and run a mission is hard work. To be part of a witness or visiting team in the local church calls for hard work. Leading youth groups and really pastoring teenagers into the kingdom calls for faithfulness and patience. Evangelism is always with people who are not, initially, on your side – that can be stressful.

'Some of us,' said the Bishop of Leicester to me as we talked about Mission England, 'have got to get our noses blooded in evangelism!'

But there is another sort of activity which is also hard work. *Evangelism small or large has got to start with prayer*. When we started Mission England we believed God was saying, 'Get the churches on their knees before anything else!' I believe that is still God's message to his people.

Who cares for the nation? Who feels the sort of distress Paul felt in Athens? How many of us have wept for our fellow countrymen as Jesus did as he entered Jerusalem?

If we really care about reaching our nation for Christ it will make us pray.

If we really care about reaching our nation for Christ it will make us work – and work hard for the cause of the Gospel.

If we really care about reaching our nation for Christ it will make us rearrange our priorities as denominations, congregations or just plain, ordinary people. The biggest and most profound part of this rearrangement is that it will force us to be people who are turned outwards to the world for most of the time. This is not always very comfortable – incarnation rarely is. If evangelism, however, is ever to happen we have no other option. Let the words of Sam Shoemaker, the American pastor and evangelist, close this book.

I stand by the door
I neither go too far in, nor stay too far out,
The door is the most important door in the world –
It is the door through which men walk when they find God.

Men die outside that door, as starving beggars die
On cold nights in cruel cities in the dead of winter –
Die for want of what is within their grasp.
Nothing else matters compared to helping them find it,
And open it, and walk in, and find Him . . .
So I stand by the door.

Some must inhabit those inner rooms,
And know the depths and heights of God,
And call outside to the rest of us how wonderful it is.
Sometimes I take a deeper look in,
Sometimes venture in a little farther;
But my place seems closer to the opening . . .
So I stand by the door.

Who Cares?

I admire the people who go way in.
But I wish they would not forget how it was
Before they got in. Then they would be able to help
The people who have not yet even found the door.

As for me, I shall take my old accustomed place,
Near enough to God to hear him, and know he is there,
But not so far from men as *not* to hear *them*
And remember they are there, too.
Where? Outside the door –
Thousands of them, millions of them.
But – more important for me –
One of them, two of them, ten of them,
Whose hands I am intended to put on the latch.
So I shall stand by the door and wait
For those who seek it.
'I had rather be a door-keeper . . .'
So I stand by the door.[1]

---

[1] From 'I stand by the door', © Helen Smith Shoemaker (Word Books, Waco, Texas).

IS THE NEW TESTAMENT HISTORY?

Paul Barnett

Foreword by F F Bruce

At the heart of the Christian faith lie a number of key events, recorded in the Gospel texts.

But can we believe the writings of a few 'biased' early Christians? Have we anything else to go on? Were any of the writers eye-witnesses? And can we be sure that their writings were not altered or distorted by later generations?

Dry history and archive research come alive as Paul Barnett answers these and other questions, showing how standard methods of historical research can be used to cross-check New Testament documents against those of non-Christian historians of the period.

Including something of his own experience as a seeker and then as a follower of Jesus, Dr Barnett makes no demands on a sceptical reader to believe 'blindly' – only to be informed of the historical facts. IS THE NEW TESTAMENT HISTORY? will also increase the confidence of Christians in the foundation of their faith.

The Rev Dr Paul Barnett is Master of Tober Menzies College, Macquarie University, Sydney.

ANGELS: GOD'S SECRET AGENTS

Billy Graham

Revised and expanded edition

The supernatural is widely accepted as fact today, yet the emphasis seems to be on the occult and the forces of evil. But what of the forces of good? Many doubt the existence of angels, yet the Bible mentions them nearly three hundred times.

In this expanded edition Billy Graham shares his discoveries about angels in the Scriptures and affirms that angels have a positive, life enhancing role to play in the lives of God's people.

'This sensational bestseller about the supernatural good deserves to be pondered by all . . . the theme is of universal religious significance. The Bible is as full of angels as it is of demons.'

Church Times

THE CASE AGAINST CHRIST

John Young

New and fully revised edition

What keeps people in the Church? Is Christianity worth investigating? In response to such questions, John Young provides a defence of the Christian faith for atheists, agnostics, enquirers – and Christians.

'This is a fantastic little paperback.'

Buzz

'It is a remarkable achievement to have combined a lively entertaining style with genuine scholarship, and a robust personal faith with openness to the objections and criticisms which may be urged against Christianity.'

Stuart Blanch, from his foreward

'The Devil has had a field day with the prejudiced assumption that you have to be some sort of moron to swallow Christianity. This little book does much to set the record straight and to demonstrate that, far from being in conflict, Christian faith goes hand in hand with reason, common sense, and historical fact.'

Cliff Richard

John Young is chaplain at the College of Ripon and York St. John.